The Story of Chinese Books

Written by Liu Guojun and Zheng Rusi
Translated by Zhou Yicheng

FOREIGN LANGUAGES PRESS   BEIJING

First Edition   1985

ISBN 0-8351-1304-3

Edited and Published by Foreign Languages Press
24 Baiwanzhuang Road, Beijing, China

Printed by Foreign Languages Printing House
19 West Chegongzhuang Road, Beijing, China

Distributed by China International Book Trading Corporation
(Guoji Shudian), P.O. Box 399, Beijing, China

Printed in the People's Republic of China

Oracle bone inscription
from the Shang Dynasty

Bamboo strip from the
Warring States Period

Ming wen (inscribed writing) on
a Zhou Dynasty bronze vessel

Da Yu tripod of the Zhou Dynasty

Rubbing from the Da Yu tripod inscription

Fragment of a stone classic carved during the
Xiping reign of the Eastern Han Dynasty

Bamboo strips unearthed from a Han tomb

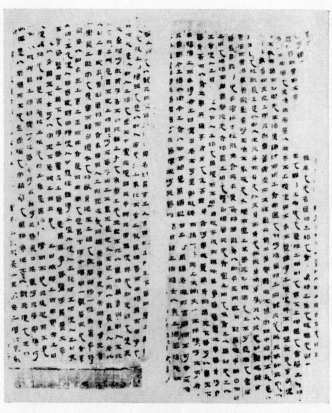

A part of *The Book of Lao Zi* (Edition B) written on silk fabrics, unearthed from a Han tomb

The world's oldest extant printed book, the *Diamond Sutra* of the Tang Dynasty

佛說是經巳長老湏菩提及諸比丘比丘尼優
婆塞優婆夷一切世間天人阿修羅聞佛所說
皆大歡喜信受奉行

金剛般若波羅蜜經

真言

那謨婆伽　跋帝　鉢喇若　波羅蜜多曳

唵　伊唎帝　伊失唎　戍嚧馱　毗舍耶　毗舍耶

婆婆訶

咸通九年四月十五日王玠為

二親敬造普施

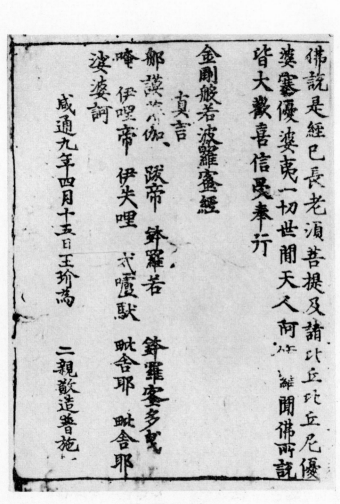

The *Diamond Sutra*

Song Dynasty block-printed *Zuo Qiuming's Commentary on "The Spring and Autumn Annals"* (in butterfly binding)

Southern Song block-printed poems by Yu Xuanji of the Tang Dynasty

白氏文集卷之七

題潯陽樓

常愛陶彭澤，文思何高玄。又恠韋江州，詩情亦清閑。今朝登此樓，有以知其然。大江寒見底，匡山青倚天。深夜湓浦月，平旦爐峰煙。清輝與靈氣，日夕供文篇。我無二人才，孰為來其間。因高偶成句，俯仰愧江山。

訪陶公舊宅并序

予夙慕陶淵明為人，往歲渭川閑居，嘗有效陶體詩十六首。今遊廬山，經柴桑，過栗里，思其人，訪其宅，不能默默，又題此詩云。

垢塵不污玉，靈鳳不啄羶。嗚呼陶靖節，生彼晉宋間。心實有所守，口終不能言。永惟孤竹子，拂衣首陽山。夷齊各一身，窮餓未為難。先生有五男，與之同飢寒。腸中食不充，身上衣不完。連徵竟不起，斯可謂貞賢。

Specimen of Bai Juyi's *Anthology*, printed by movable copper type during the Ming Dynasty

渡江

庚申秋日王文衡寫

Ming Dynasty woodcut picture printing

Contents

Foreword

Books have played an important role in the history of mankind. With each stage of development in human society, books have become even more important in people's lives, and today they are playing a still greater role in society. But it has taken a long time for books to become what they are today.

The Chinese book has a history of over 3,600 years, an interesting history and one full of anecdotes.

Before paper was invented, people of different nations throughout the world inscribed their messages on a great variety of materials. Stone, reeds, wax plates and parchment were used by Europeans. Baked clay was used by the Babylonians. Pattra was used by the Indians. And tortoise shells, bones, bronze, stone, bamboo strips and wooden slats and silk were used by the Chinese.

The materials that were used determined the size and form of Chinese books. A "book" carved on stone might be several metres high and more than a metre wide, while each strip of bamboo or each slat of wood in a book measured about a third of a metre in length and one or two centimetres in width. A silk scroll was usually a third of a metre high and several metres long.

Before they were printed by modern methods, Chinese books were carved, incised and copied by hand. Inscriptions carved or incised on the surface of shells and bones are known as "books on tortoise shells and animal bones".

The earliest ones date back to the Shang Dynasty (c. 16th-11th centuries B.C.). As they recorded statements of oracles received by slave owners and were not meant for repeated reading and studying, they are not books in the ordinary sense.

In the 13th and 14th centuries B.C., the ancient Chinese began to carve or cast inscriptions on bronze ware, and thus they produced "books on bronze". For example, the famous Da Yu *ding* (tripod), cast early in the Western Zhou Dynasty (c. 11th century-770 B.C.), records the fact that a nobleman was rewarded by the king with land, clothing, chariots, horses and a large number of slaves.

Inscriptions carved on stone tablets are often called "books of stone". The earliest one was carved in A.D. 175, the fourth year of the reign of Xiping of the Eastern Han Dynasty (A.D. 25-220). The tablet was inscribed with Confucian classics and placed outside the Imperial Academy in the city of Luoyang so that everybody could read it.

Words carved on stone or bronze are not books in the regular sense, of course, but they played the role of books. The first real book appeared in China at the end of the Spring and Autumn Period (770-476 B.C.). It was called a *jian ce*, or bamboo book, and was written with a brush on strips of bamboo or slats of wood. More than 4,900 such bamboo strips were retrieved during an excavation at Yinqueshan, Shandong, in 1972. The writings on the bamboo strips are copies of classics written before the Qin Dynasty (221-207 B.C.), including works such as *Sun Wu's Art of War, Sun Bin's Art of War, The Book of Weiliao Zi, Six Strategies, The Book of Guan Zi* and *The Book of Yan Zi*. The most significant of these is *Sun Bin's Art of War,* which had been considered lost for more than 1,000 years.

Books were written not only on bamboo strips but also on scrolls of silk fabric. More than 20 books on such silk scrolls, totalling 100,000 characters, were discovered in 1973 in a Han Dynasty tomb at Mawangdui near Changsha, Hunan Province. Among them were a number of lost books, the most valuable of which were two editions of *The Book of Lao Zi*. At the end of Edition A and the beginning of Edition B were four previously unknown articles omitted from existing editions of the book.

The invention of paper in the 1st century A.D. and the spread of paper-making techniques constituted an important contribution made by the working people of ancient China to the cultural development of the world. When paper replaced the clumsy bamboo strips and expensive silk, the production of books developed rapidly. After that, Chinese books were designed in the form of scrolls. Damaged scrolls of the *History of the Three Kingdoms,* hand-copied in the 4th century during the Jin Dynasty, were discovered in Xinjiang in 1924 as well as in 1965. These are the oldest rolls of manuscripts to be found in China.

The invention of block printing in China, around the 8th century, and of movable-type printing in the 11th century were two more important contributions of the ancient Chinese working people to world civilization. The earliest printed matter extant in the world is the *Diamond Sutra,* printed in 868, during the ninth year of the Xiantong reign of the Tang Dynasty.

After the invention of printing, the number of Chinese books greatly increased and their subjects covered a far greater range than before. *History as a Mirror,* compiled by Sima Guang in the Song Dynasty (960-1279), is an outstanding book of chronological history. The *Taiping Imperial*

Encyclopedia, Choice Blossoms from the Garden of Literature, Taiping Miscellany and *Encyclopedia of History*, all compiled during the Northern Song period (960-1127), are known as the four great books of the Song Dynasty. The *Taiping Imperial Encyclopedia* alone constitutes 1,000 fascicles of classified entries. The *Yongle Encyclopedia* of the Ming Dynasty (1368-1644), however, was the largest set of books compiled in ancient China. Comprising 22,877 fascicles, a table of contents of 60 fascicles, and bound in 11,095 volumes, it is the largest encyclopedia ever produced in the world. The *Compendium of Materia Medica*, written by Li Shizhen during the Ming Dynasty, is a world-famous pharmacopoeia. *The Complete Library of the Four Treasures of Knowledge*, compiled during the Qian Long period of the Qing Dynasty (1644-1911), is a gigantic collection of 3,503 titles in 79,337 fascicles.

Most of these works were printed and have been handed down through the centuries to the present day. Some, however, consisted of only one or several manuscript copies, because they had too many volumes to be printed by woodblocks. A number of these works have only a few volumes remaining. The rest were lost in wars and other disasters.

After the introduction of modern mechanical printing from Europe into China in the early 19th century, book publication underwent momentous changes. The traditional Chinese handicraft method of printing was gradually replaced by modern letterpress, lithographic and photogravure techniques, using machines and automatic printing presses.

This book, *The Story of Chinese Books*, tells how books emerged, developed and changed in China. It was first published in 1958. This second edition was revised by

the authors, and includes information on recently unearthed archeological materials. It also includes extensive sup-
plements and revisions concerning the origin of books in
China, particularly in terms of the history and development of printing, block making and the systemization of
books.

Chapter I

Origin of Written Chinese and Books

Some form of written language is essential to the formation of books; without a written language there could be no books. Therefore the first thing we need to discuss is how China came to have a written language.

People in the remote past had no written language. Historians refer to this time in history as the "Prehistoric Period" of social development, a time when people still lived in clan communes and used spoken language as their only means of exchanging ideas. Spoken language can be heard only a short distance away, and the sound vanishes the moment it is produced. Words spoken a minute ago are no longer heard, and utterances made yesterday or the day before may soon be forgotten.

As society developed, it became very necessary for people to keep records of their experiences and the experiences of others, and to know about events of the past and happenings in faraway places. The only way to keep such records was to memorize them. By using words and phrases that could easily be memorized, people preserved their ideas and knowledge in songs, ballads, proverbs, stories and idioms. Later generations then memorized these sayings and songs word by word and sentence by sentence so that they could be recited when necessary.

Thus records were imparted from one generation to another, and from one area in the world to another. Through folktales people were able to know something of the life and thinking of earlier generations and something about the state of things in other places. People endowed with good memories came to know many folktales and played a major role as disseminators of culture, or "living books".

Thus much of the knowledge we have from ancient times was preserved in this way, as were many priceless literary and artistic works. The *Iliad* and *Odyssey* are examples of two world famous greek epics that were handed down for many generations by Greek folk singers. Some of the poems in the *Chu Ci* (*Elegies of Chu*)* were also preserved in this manner. Stories about some Chinese legendary figures, such as You Chao, Sui Ren, Fu Xi and Shen Nong, were also handed down by folk singers. Even after written language came into use, many Confucian classics were still preserved by word of mouth during the Qin Dynasty (221-206 B.C.) and Han Dynasty (206 B.C.- A.D. 220).

But the drawback in this method of preserving records is that human memories are not always reliable. When words are repeated omissions occur, and additions are sometimes made. With the passage of time, ancient folktales often changed greatly from their original forms. We therefore cannot take for granted data preserved in old folktales.

Because memories are fallible, people devised various ways to help their memories; objects were used to assist

---

* *Chu Ci* is an anthology of poems from ancient China, most of which were written by Qu Yuan (c. 340-278 B.C.).

2

recollection. Noteworthy was the method of tying knots. Different knots — large or small, single or multiple, tied in various colours and placed high or low on a rope — indicated different things. Many ancient peoples used this method, including the Chinese. We know this because there is a saying, "recording things by tying knots in olden times," written in the *Yi Jing* (*The Book of Changes*) and other classical works. However we know nothing of what these knots meant to the ancient Chinese or their method of tying knots. But among the various nationalities of China, such as the Lisus and Hanis in Yunnan and the Gaoshans in Taiwan, tying knots as an aid to memory was still in vogue fairly recently. When the Hani people bought or sold land, they put knots in a single strand of rope to indicate the value of the plots. Duplicate strands were given to both sides as evidence of the transaction. In other countries the practice is also known. The Tatars, Persians, Mexicans and Peruvians all used this method of tying knots at one time.

Cutting marks in wood was also a method used by ancient people to aid their memories. They cut different signs on the wood to indicate different things. It goes without saying that our forefathers must have also used this memory-aid method. This is shown by "notched wood strips" that have been found in some of our oldest books. The method was also used by some of China's minority peoples. In the Museum of Yunnan Province there is a notched log once preserved by the Va people. On both sides of the log are an assortment of markings, the deep notches indicating big events and shallow notches indicating small ones. Each year in the past new notches were added to the log. Every year at harvest time, villagers old and young gathered for meal at which a respected elder told them of the significance of the different notches. Thus they recalled the events that had taken place in their village, and the feuds their predecessors had been engaged in with other villages. Occasions like this preserved the collective memory of the Va people as an unbroken line.

Tying knots and putting notches in wood strips were forerunners of books. Knots and pieces of wood were easy to carry and they could be preserved for posterity. They made up for the lack of a written language for those who knew the secrets of the knots or row of notches. Since such knots and notches were only memory aids, they were not language signs and did not constitute a written language. Written language, as it turns out, evolved instead from drawing pictures.

Ancient people drew pictures of animal hunting and other things closely related to their productive labour on the rock walls of their cave dwellings. Typical examples are Paleolithic drawings found in the caves at Zhoukoudian in China and in caves of France and Spain. These pictures are so vivid and true to life that people today marvel at their intricacy. From such art works surely arose the concept of expressing ideas by pictures rather than by notches or knots. After a deer or an ox has been drawn, one knows what the picture stands for in a way that is impossible with a knot in a rope.

At first, the pictures used as writing were accurate representations of the subject. But, in time, they became simplified and were reproduced with just a few simple lines or strokes. Pictures then stood as signs for words, and were sometimes totally detached from pictures of actual things. This was the most primitive form of written script, known as picture-written language or pictographs.

The present-day Chinese written script certainly

evolved from such pictographs. Our forefathers began to use them 4,000 to 5,000 years ago, in the late period of primitive commune, i.e., during the period of the Yangshao Culture (in modern Mianchi County, Henan) in the matriarchal clan commune society of 4115-2065 B.C. and the period of the Longshan Culture (in modern Licheng County, Shandong) in the patriarchal clan commune society of 1725-1695 B.C. In due course black and multi-coloured pottery with sign-scripts on it, some in single words and some in whole sentences, was discovered in archeological excavations. As the signs were inscribed on the pottery they are known as inscribed writing. During the course of an excavation at the site of the capital of the Shang Dynasty in Jiangxi Province, an excavation conducted from 1973 to 1974, inscribed writings and script-signs on pottery and stone slabs were also unearthed.

Studies by archeologists suggest that these script-signs and inscribed writings are closely related to the appearance and formation of written Chinese. As they have many similarities to the later oracle bone inscriptions and inscriptions on bronzes of the Shang Dynasty, some people believe they were precursors of the country's written script. But archeologists do not agree on this matter, and more archeological data are needed before a difinitive conclusion can be reached.

With the development of social production and class polarization, the embryonic form of the state appeared. After the emergence of the state, people of the ruling class, especially those at the top, found themselves in need of a better way to keep records in carrying out state affairs. Writing as a means of record keeping thus developed at this time, and all the written scripts and records were under the exclusive control and use of the slave owners

5

and nobility.   The earliest written records found in China are those of the Shang Dynasty, 3,500 years ago, a period when the country was under a slave system.

Chapter II

Oracle Bone, Bronze and Stone Inscriptions

Oracle Bone Inscriptions

The earliest Chinese writing is the *jia gu wen* (oracle bone inscriptions) which dates back to the later part of the Shang (Yin) Dynasty (c. 14th-11th centuries B.C.). The oracle bones were first discovered in Xiaotun Village, Anyang County, Henan Province, in 1899. Unidentified and few in number at first, they were sold as fossil fragments to people who used them in brewing traditional Chinese medicine. Later they came to the attention of Chinese scholars who realized that they were inscribed with ancient writings. After much study and deciphering, the scholars established the fact that they were the writings of the Shang Dynasty, and recorded events of that time. They thus offered valuable material for research into the history of the Shang Dynasty. The writings were inscribed on the carapaces of tortoises and on mammals' bones for purposes of divination and so they became known as oracle bones. After more were found in the excavation at the old site of the capital of the Yin Dynasty, they also became known as the writing of the Yin ruins.

Shang Dynasty writing carved
on the carapace of a tortoise

The ancient script is so different in form from our
present writing that a layman can make nothing of it. The
greater part of the inscriptions are pictographs, often
without any fixed form. The same character may be written
in as many as a dozen different ways. Some of the oracle-
bone signs are complicated pictures, others are made with
only a few strokes. Yet they include pictophonetic and
phonetic loan characters that are inserted according to fixed
grammatical rules. This leads us to believe that this form
of written language had been in use for a long period of
time. As most of the shells and bones were broken, it is

difficult to tell whether they had any set number of characters or size. Indications are that they had no other form than the one provided by the natural object — a whole carapace or whole bone, large or small — and an inscription might consist of one column of characters or as many as ten columns. Apparently there was no set limit.

As we have said, the oracle bones were used for divination. They contain the records of questions asked of the gods or of divine ancestors. The superstitious and unscientific practice of divination was deep-rooted among the ancient Shangs. Before going into a battle or on a tour of inspection, offering sacrifices, or in cases of sickness and poor harvests, the Shang emperors sought divine guidance. The shells and bones are invariably marked with the date of the year, month and day; the reasons for seeking guidance; the names of people seeking it, and the interpretations of the subsequent divine instructions which were kept for later verification. Since the Shangs valued these records, they preserved them carefully. Thanks to their preservation, we have been able to unearth them 3,000 years later. The site where the largest number of oracle bones have been found was most probably the royal storeroom in which they were kept.

The writing on the oracle bones reveals the conditions in China from about 1300 B.C. to 1100 B.C. Through these finds, we have come to know much of the history, politics, military and economic affairs, customs and habits, and social organization of the Shang Dynasty.

Oracle bone inscriptions were the earliest Chinese writings. But bones like these cannot be called books. They were only brief messages used for divination. They were not intended to disseminate historical knowledge or to be studied.

Bronze Inscriptions

Beginning in the 14th and 13th centuries B.C., our forefathers also cast characters in, or inscribed characters on, bronze. This practice began with the appearance of private ownership. People in these ancient times inscribed their names or symbols on tools and weapons to denote their ownership. This was a transitional period from primitive communism to private ownership, and it is known as the Bronze Age. Archeologists do not agree on the exact period when bronze came into use in China. But it was probably during the middle period of the Shang Dynasty, about the 14th century B.C. By then private ownership and states based on a slave system were well established.

Bronze articles, being favourite possessions, were inscribed with a name or other symbols to show ownership. Later they were inscribed with writing to commemorate a special occasion or to explain particular reasons for making a specific bronze article. Other inscriptions described their use and recorded the names of the makers. Still later, the practice of preserving writings of great importance by inscribing them on bronzes came into use. The number of characters inscribed on bronze articles then increased from one or two to hundreds. They became commonly known as *ming wen* or inscribed writings. These commemorative writings give us much information about historical events, and they were, in a way, the first written records.

The period of bronze inscriptions lasted from the middle-half period of the Shang Dynasty to the early Eastern Han Dynasty (A.D. 25-220), i.e., from the 14th century B.C. to the 1st century A.D. Of these, the inscrip-

Food vessel from the Western Zhou Dynasty

tions of the Zhou Dynasty (1066-256 B.C.) provide the greatest documentary value because they verify and supplement later written historical records.

The style of *ming wen* varied at different times and in different places, but none of them resembled writing today. These characters were also called *zhong ding wen* (writing on bronze bells or tripods) and included several styles. The earliest was like the oracle bone writings and the latest were *xiao zhuan* (small seal characters) and *li shu* (official script). During the Spring and Autumn Period (770-476 B.C.) and the Warring States Period (476-

11

221 B.C.), each of the states — Qi, Chu, Qin, etc. — had its own style of writing engraved on bronzes. These various styles, when arranged in chronological order and according to the places where each was practised, offer excellent material for research into the development of Chinese characters.

Most of the bronze articles had *ming wen* cast on them when they were made, but some had the writing inscribed afterwards. A bronze container could have *ming wen* cast or inscribed on its body or inside of the lid. The writing on most of the bronze containers and their lids bore the same content. The types of bronze articles covered a wide range and included such objects as a *ding* (tripod), *zun* (wine vessel), *hu* (jug), *pan* (tray or plate), *yu* (jar), *fu* (food vessel), *yin* (bell), *dun* (grain receptacle) and *you* (wine vessel). The bronzes used by the ruling class in feasting or as objects for offering sacrifices to the gods and ancestors were given the name *li qi* (ceremonial vessels) or *ji jin* (metals of blessing). Musical instruments and weapons were also among those bronze objects that had *ming wen* cast or inscribed on them. But these generally bore fewer characters than the metals of blessing, which usually had 300 to 400 characters inscribed on them.

The San Shi *pan* (tray), Guo Ji Zi Bai *pan* (tray), Mao Gong *ding* (tripod) and Hu *ding* bear long inscriptions, and are important objects for research into the history of the Western Zhou Dynasty (c. 11th century-771 B.C.). The Hu *ding*, for example, which was made in the middle period of the Western Zhou Dynasty, records a transaction between two slave dealers who trade one horse and a bolt of silk for five slaves. On the well-known Da Yu *ding* made in early Western Zhou times, there is a record of a man named Yu who received land and grants of a

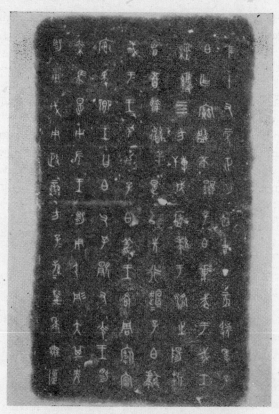

Inscribed writing on the Guo Ji Zi Bai
pan (bronze tray), Western Zhou Dynasty

chariot and horses, clothing and a horde of slaves. In the
Palace Museum of Beijing, the Museum of Chinese History, the Archeological Institute of the Chinese Academy
of Sciences and the Nanjing Museum there are large collections of bronzes that have come down from ancient times.

13

These will continue to contribute to our academic studies for a long time to come.

The bronzes are not only valuable for their inscribed writings, but their casting, design and decorative patterns provide us with priceless material for the study of arts and crafts in ancient China. In fact they are treasured among the world's finest works of art of that time.

The bronzes, of course, had their own useful purpose as sacrificial or ceremonial vessels, and the inscribed writing was in a sense incidental. These, like the oracle bones, were not books. But by this time books had already made their appearance in a simple, primitive form.

Stone Inscriptions

Before we deal with the subject of books in the normal sense, we need to say something about stone inscriptions.

Although primitive people drew pictures on stone, it was only after the invention of written languages that there was the possibility of people inscribing writing on stones. Many other people, such as the Egyptians and Red Indians, inscribed writings on stone early in their history. But in China no such stone has as yet been found. The earliest engraved stones that have been found in China are 10 stone drums of the Qin Dynasty. Carved all over these drums is a poem singing the praises of hunting. The characters are carved in a style like that of the *xiao zhuan* (small seal characters) of the Qin state. Though there is still no agreement as to the exact date or year when the poem was carved on the stone drums, it is generally agreed that they were commissioned by Duke Wen of the Qin state, during the reign of King Ping of the Zhou Dynasty. This was prior to the Warring States Period.

The practice of inscribing characters on stone might have been used during the Spring and Autumn Period, since there was a statement written in the book *Mo Zi* of the early Warring States Period that says, "Engrave on metal or stone" in a description about how to preserve written records. Since we know that there was inscribed writing on bronzes during the Spring and Autumn Period, it is probable that this statement about there being inscribed writing on stone must also be true. But apart from the stone drums there are no other engraved stones from this early period. Then there were the stone inscriptions of the Qin Dynasty (221-201 B.C.) when the first emperor of the Qin Dynasty made an inspection tour of the land after his unification of the country.

During the Han Dynasty (206 B.C.-A.D. 220) it was common to inscribe writing on stone. This was done in various ways during the Eastern Han Dynasty. Some inscriptions were put on rock cliffs. These are known as rock inscriptions. Others were put on rectangular and round monoliths that were set up for viewing in open fields. These are known as tablets and steles. The writing on them commemorated military exploits, travels or construction projects. Some steles also contained biographies of noted individuals. The Ode to Xixia, Ode to Shimen, Tablet to Zhao Kuan and Tablet to Gengxun are steles that were produced during the Eastern Han Dynasty. Though these provide material for historical research, their main purpose was commemoration or commendation. They were not books in the normal sense.

The year A.D. 175, during the reign of the Eastern Han emperor Ling Di, was probably when the first whole text of a book was inscribed on stone for the public to read. The emperor saw to it that the full texts of the *Shu Jing* (*The Book of History*), *Shi Jing* (*The Book of Songs*), *Yi Jing* (*The Book of Changes*), *Yi Li* (*The Book of Rites*), *Chun Qiu* (*The Spring and Autumn Annals*), *Chun Qiu Gong Yang Zhuan* (*Gong Yang's Commentary on "The Spring and Autumn Annals"*), and *Lun Yu* (*Analects of Confucius*), inscribed on stone in the famous calligraphy of Chai Yong. The emperor had these inscribed stones

Rubbing from a stone inscription of the Han Dynasty

erected in front of the Imperial Academy at Luoyang so that they could be studied by all persons who could read.

Paper had been invented by then, but it was not yet widely used for books, and printing was still unknown. The only way to make duplicate copies was by hand. The books of that time consisted mainly of writing on bamboo strips (see Chapter III). Errors frequently occurred at each copying. Students and scholars were therefore distressed at being unable to secure accurate copies of texts. The erection of the stone tablets met a timely need. First, errors that occurred in hand-copying could thus be avoided. Second, rubbings could be made from the stone inscriptions. These replaced hand-copying and were faster to reproduce. They helped to open the way for the invention of printing.

During the Zhengshi reign (A.D. 240-248) of the Wei Kingdom, the *Gu Wen Sheng Shu* (*Book of History in Ancient Script*) and a part of the *Chun Qiu Zuo Shi Zhuan* (*Zuo Qiuming's Commentary on "The Spring and Autumn Annals"*) were inscribed on stone in an ancient script of the pre-Qin Dynasty style, in "small seal characters" and in "official script". Erected at the Imperial Academy of Luoyang, these became known as "the three-style stone classics."

During the Kaicheng reign (A.D. 836-840) of Emperor Wen Zong of the Tang Dynasty (A.D. 618-907) *kai shu* (regular style) was used to inscribe the 12 Confucian classics — *Yi Jing, Shu Jing, Yi Li, Shi Jing, Zhou Li* (*Rites of the Zhou Dynasty*), *Li Ji* (*Records of Rites*), *Chun Qiu Zuo Shi Zhuan, Chun Qiu Gong Yang Zhuan, Chun Qiu Gu Liang Zhuan* (*Gu Liang's Commentary on "The Spring and Autumn Annals"*), *Xiao Jing* (*The Canon of Filial Piety*), *Lun Yu* and *Er Ya* (*Literary Expositor*) — on stone. The emperor had these erected at the Imperial Academy of Chang'an (now Xi'an). With the invention of printing about this time, Confucian classics began to be printed by woodblocks copied from these stone classics. During the subsequent Northern Song (960-1127) and Southern Song (1127-1279) dynasties, and under the reign of Emperor Qian Long (1736-1795) of the Qing Dynasty (1644-1911), there were other stone inscriptions erected that contained classic writings.

Stone tablets served a useful purpose in that rubbings,

a predecessor of printing, could be made from them. The rubbings eventually led to block printing since the rubbings were done by pressing paper onto the stone and covering it with ink. Because the ink only touched the raised portions of the stone and not the incised characters, the text of a rubbing would appear white against a black background. A few hundred years later stone carvers began to cut characters in relief and in reverse so that they would have raised surfaces that would print in black after inking. Thus, block printing came into being with black characters on a white background.

In summary, oracle bone inscriptions and inscriptions on bronzes provide the oldest written records in China. They were used for official documents of dynastic rulers and for their personal records and not for the dissemination of knowledge. Thus oracle bones and bronzes can in no way be regarded as books in the normal sense. Although some stone steles contained the texts of books, these were inscribed long after the development of handwritten books, the subject of the next chapter.

Chapter III

Writings on Bamboo Strips and Wooden Slats
The *Jian Ce* System

The oldest books in China were written on bamboo strips or wooden slats. And bamboo and wood were the earliest materials used in China for book making.

Books on bamboo strips were known by the ancients as *jian ce* (简策), while those on wooden slats were called *ban du* (版牍). When speaking of a book or books, people at that time used the words *dian ce* (典册), *dian ji* (典籍), *jian bian* (简编) and *fang ce* (方策) indiscriminately to refer a book or books made of bamboo strips or wooden slats. This is shown, for example, in the *Zhong Yong* (*Doctrine of the Mean*), where it says, "Written all over the *fang ce* is the philosophy of King Wen and King Wu," meaning that the arguments and principles of King Wen and King Wu of the Zhou Dynasty were recorded in books of that time. The *Zhong Yong* was a representative work of the Warring States Period. *Jian ce* was then so commonly used as the general name and common form of old books that it by itself had led people to know the *jian ce* system.

Books made of bamboo strips and wooden slats were in use earlier than the Warring States Period. They probably existed during the Shang Dynasty. In fact it has long been said that, "it was the Shangs who began to use *dian*

19

and *ce*", i.e., *dian ce*, *dian ji*, etc. The character 册 (ce) has even been found on some of the Shang oracle bones. By the Zhou Dynasty *ce, dian* and the like were widely used. Clear evidence shows that *jian ce* was regarded as the main form of book making from the Warring States Period to the late Eastern Han Dynasty.

But no *jian ce* written by the ancient Chinese has survived. Though there are historical records of the discovery of ancient *jian ce,* none of these still exist.

Over the last 80 years, in southern Xinjiang, at Yumenguan in the Dunhuang area of Gansu and in the vicinity of Lake Juyan in Eqina Banner of Inner Mongolia, a large number of *jian du* (简牍) have been found. These originated between the 2nd century B.C. and A.D. 4th century, and have given us a picture of the times in which these objects were used. The majority contained official documents related to the country's border areas. One was an inventory showing the number of arms, instruments and other articles in use at a far-off military post between

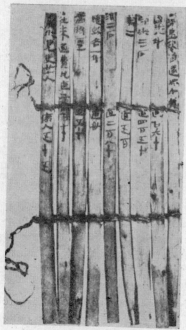

Recording strips with the number of weapons listed

A.D. 93 and 95. It was formed of 77 wooden slats, which were somewhat decomposed and broken, but the cords that tied them together still held fast. The subject matter of this *jian ce,* an official record, discloses the secrecy of most *jian ce,* and the fact that it was made of wood suggests that when there was a lack of bamboo, thin strips of wood were used. *Jian ce* thus could be made either of bamboo strips or wooden slats. But in either case they were made in the same shape and strung together in the same way. Written records made of wooden slats have also been found in southern Xinjiang, a number of which were written in minority nationality languages. Each of these *ban*

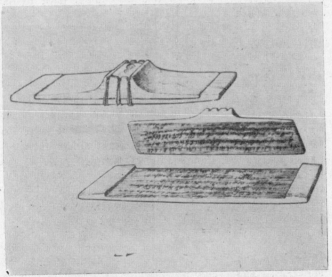

Ban du (writing on wooden slats) of the Han Dynasty

du was written on two separate slats, one notched into the other, cord-bound and affixed with a seal. The writing is composed of correspondence and contracts or deeds of that time. The material is highly valued for research into the history of Xinjiang extending back to the Han Dynasty.

After the founding of the People's Republic of China, archeologists discovered ancient bamboo strips at a number of different sites. They were found in 1951, in an old tomb on Zuogongshan Mountain in Changsha, and again in 1953, in another old tomb at Lake Yangtian in Changsha. In both cases the bamboo strips dated back to the Kingdom of Chu during the Warring States Period. In 1957, in an old tomb at Changtaiguan in Xinyang, Henan Province, bamboo strips were found that also dated back to the Warring States Period. And in 1959, in an old tomb in Wuwei, Gansu Province, 370 bamboo strips were found that date back to the early Eastern Han Dynasty. The text on these is part of the old book *Yi Li*. It includes seven sections of the original 17. Initial research shows that the characters written on these bamboo strips were done in the hand of a certain calligrapher living during the late years of the Western Han Dynasty. The bamboo strips are still in good shape, though the strings holding them together had rotted. Examination of the text corrected the mistaken view that the writing on old bamboo strips was incised into the bamboo or done with varnish instead of ink and a brush.

In recent years archeologists have found more and more bamboo strips and wooden slats in ancient burials. Included among these finds are some made of different materials. The *Treaty of Alliance,* unearthed in 1965 at the site of the capital of the state of Jin in Houma, Shanxi Province, was written in vermilion on stone and jade splints. The text was a pact that the state of Jin entered into 2,400 years ago, during the Warring States Period. It gives us a glimpse of the documentary form of written records before the country was unified under the central rule of Qin Shi Huang (First Emperor of the Qin Dynasty). The pact also provides us with data for studying the class struggle and social relations of that time, as well as the form of the written Chinese language before the time of Qin Shi Huang.

The bamboo strips and wooden slats that have been found also include the Confucian classics and works produced by exponents of various schools of thought in ancient times. The discoveries also include works on military arts, medical works, laws and regulations, almanacs and writings on divination. In addition to these, there are a number of "registering strips", or lists of burial objects.

Among the objects unearthed from Han Tomb No. 1 at Mawangdui, in Changsha, there were 312 bamboo strips. The number of characters on each strip varied. Some had two characters, some 25. Some of the texts were even punctuated. The writings and the burial articles listed on the strips have proved valuable in tracing the nomenclature of some old objects.

Treaty of alliance unearthed at Houma, Shanxi Province

23

In 1972, in a Han Dynasty tomb at Wuwei, Gansu Province, a bast-fibre satchel was unearthed. It contained 90 wooden slats with medical writings on them. Furthermore, from Han Tomb No. 2 at Mawangdui, in Changsha, there was unearthed an almanac dating back to the Yuan-guang reign (129 B.C.) of the Han Dynasty Emperor Wu Di. This is the earliest and the most complete almanac so far found in China.

Of particular interest is the find in a tomb of the early Western Han Dynasty on Yingqueshan Mountain in Linyi, Shandong Province. Here were unearthed a large number of pre-Qin Dynasty classics, altogether in 4,900 bamboo strips. Among these were included *Sun Zi Bing Fa* (*Sun Wu's Art of War*), *Sun Bin Bing Fa* (*Sun Bin's Art of War*), *Wei Liao Zi* (*The Book of Weiliao Zi*), *Liu Tao* (*Six Strategies*), *Guan Zi* (*The Book of Guan Zi*) and *Yan Zi* (*The Book of Yan Zi*). Considered lost for more than 1,000 years, *Sun Bin's Art of War* is of great textual signif-icance. It was listed in "Chapter on Biography" of the *History of the Han Dynasty* by Ban Gu, but no copy ex-isted. According to the catalogue listing, there were two books on military arts. Ban Gu gave the name *Wu Sun Zi* (*Master Sun of Wu*) to Sun Wu's treatise and *Qi Sun Zi* (*Master Sun of Qi*) to Sun Bin's.* Since both were lost, only the catalogue entry remained. Doubts as to the validity of the entry were thus raised among scholars. Some believed that *Sun Wu's Art of War* was a forged book, passed off as an ancient one. Others presumed that it had originated in Sun Wu, and credited Sun Bin with the completion of the project. There were still others who

---

* Sun Wu was a guest minister to the Prince of the state of Wu while Sun Bin was chief of staff of the state of Qi. Hence the distinc-tion between the two masters.

24

claimed the works of the two authors were one and the same. But now, with *Sun Wu's Art of War* and *Sun Bin's Art of War* being unearthed from the same tomb, the historical riddle has been solved.

Sun Wu's Art of War and *Sun Bin's Art of War*, unearthed at Yinqueshan

In 1975, in a tomb of the Qin Dynasty at Shuihudi in Yunmeng County, Hubei Province, more than 1,000 bamboo strips were found. Initial deciphering and verification established the fact that these writings included documentary records of Garrison Commander Teng, stationed in Nanjun Prefecture during the 20th year (227 B.C.) of Qin Shi Huang's reign; laws and regulations promulgated by the Qin Dynasty; books on divination, and other writings covering a wide range of subjects. These bamboo strips provide us with a better understanding of the social and political conditions during the Qin Dynasty, and with examples of the old form of books that existed in the years before Emperor Qin Shi Huang set about burning books and burying Confucian scholars alive in 213-212 B.C.

The excavation of so many old bamboo strips and wooden slats has provided us with a rich knowledge of the way books of bamboo strips and wooden slats were made. The tubal trunk of bamboo was cut into short sections that were then split into narrow strips. Characters were written on these strips with a brush and ink. A single bamboo strip fashioned like this and covered with writing was called *jian* (简). A number of such strips, perforated and tied together in a bundle, was called *ce* (策,册) If wood was used, it was sawn into thin slats called *ban* (版) A *ban* with writing on it was called *ban du* (版牍)or simply *du*. The *ban* was usually square or oblong in form. A square slat with writing on it was called *fang ban* (方版).

Being easily obtainable, bamboo and wood were convenient for book making. The process, however, was not simple. Freshly cut bamboo had to be protected against wood-borers, and so the strips were dried over a fire before they were ready for writing. For wood, the surface of the slats had to be smoothed before characters could be written on them.

Only a limited number of characters could be written on a narrow, long strip of bamboo. A number of strips were, therefore, required to make a book. To facilitate reading, the strips were arranged in the sequence of the text and strung together in a bundle either by flax threads or by silk cords (such stringing was called *si bian*), or by leather thongs (such stringing was called *wei bian*). A bundle that contained a complete essay or chapter of a book was called *bian*. There is, for example, the seven-bian *Mencius*. Generally speaking, a strip book consisted of two or three *bian*, sometimes four or five. The book *Yi Li*, unearthed in Wuwei in 1959, is composed of four *bian*. The medical strips unearthed recently, also in Wuwei, consisted of three *bian*. Small triangular cuts had been made on the strips to aid in their use.

Medical writings on pieces of wood, unearthed from a Han tomb at Wuwei

Apparently some bamboo strip books were written first and then laced together with flax or silk cords. In other acses, the strips were laced together before the strips were covered with writings. But threading that came before writing was the general rule. Evidence of this was found in a bundle of 50 blank jade splints unearthed from a Warring States Period tomb in Huixian County. There were also blanks still discernible among the medical strips unearthed in Wuwei. In the case of books composed of records or inventories, the strips were laced together into a thin or thick volume after the records were completed. Found with cords draping over some of the characters on its strips, the *Yongyuan Inventory* was an example of this.

The length of the bamboo strips varied. In the Warring States Period and during the Han Dynasty, the longest strips were two feet four inches; the next longest, one foot two inches; and the shortest, eight inches. Classics were written on the longest strips during the Han Dynasty, *The Canon of Filial Piety* on shorter strips, and biographies and essays on the shortest. The laws of the state and history books compiled under the auspices of the government were

27

also written on the longest strips to characterize their importance.

The strips in a bundle were arranged in sequence, and covering the whole bundle, as a protective measure, were two strips with no writing on them. These are called "extra strips". Sometimes on the reverse side of the first "extra strip" was written the title of a chapter, and on the second, the book title. But usually the title of the chapter was written on the first strip following the extra strips.

If the bundle contained one of the chapters of a book, the book title (the big title) was written below the chapter title (the small title). Below the chapter title atop the text, there was sometimes space for the author's name.

Upon completion of the writing, all the strips were rolled into a bundle in a left-right direction, with the last strip acting as an axle. The titles on the reverse side of the "extra strips" were thus revealed for inspection. Though resembling scrolls yet not scrolls, bundles like this were called *bian* or *ce*. The *Yongyuan Inventory* was rolled up in this way, and when it was unearthed, the cords were in such good condition they seemed like new. The medical strips found in Wuwei contain the words "sundry prescriptions for curing diseases" on the tail-end strip, which had been used as the axle in rolling up the strips. A book could contain many bundles. They were wrapped in soft materials such as cloth or silk, and sometimes the bundles were put into a bag.

Writing on the bamboo strips was done with a brush and ink. When a wrong character was produced in the process of writing, it was erased and replaced by the correct one. People used to think that writing on the bamboo strips had been incised with some sort of cutting tool. But an increasing number of bamboo strips have been found that show this was not so. A brush, an inkstone, a bronze eraser and broken ink sticks were unearthed in an old tomb on Phoenix Hill at the former city site of the state of Chu in Jiangling, Hubei Province. The tomb dates back to the time of Emperor Wen Di of the

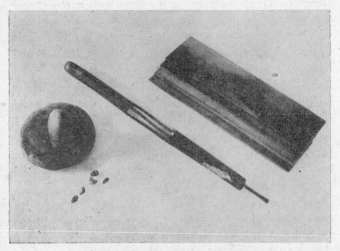

Stationery unearthed from a Han tomb

Western Han Dynasty. These finds were, in a way, a complete set of stationery for use in writing on the bamboo strips. A fine brush still in its bamboo holder with a knife, or eraser, in its wooden sheath was found in a tomb of the Qin Dynasty at Shuihudi. All these discoveries have provided sufficient evidence to show how writing was done on the old bamboo strips.

The use of wooden slats was limited to certain specific purposes, mainly for official documents, registers, notices and correspondence, as well as for drawing pictures.

Wood, in ancient times, was a material easily obtainable for correspondence. After the message was written on a slat, another one was placed on top of it. The names of the addressee and the sender of the message were written on this covering slat. The two slats acted as a primitive envelope. They were bound together with a string and clay was applied to the knot. The clay was then impressed with a seal that left the mark of characters in relief. This was called the sealing clay. Correspondence, both official and private, was done on these wooden slats.

Wooden slats were also used to write short articles and to make inventories of things. The ancient book *Yi Li* says: "Characters numbering more than a hundred are written on bamboo strips; those below a hundred are written on wooden slats." This indicates the specific use of bamboo strips for books and wooden slats for official documents and correspondence.

Books made of wood or bamboo, however, were inconvenient and unsatisfactory. They were bulky and heavy, difficult to carry, and took up a good deal of space. Every time a book was used, the strings had to be untied and then retied. Problems occurred if a string snapped and the strips became disarranged. Once the strips were disarranged, it was not easy to put them in sequence again. One or two strips might then be missing or have been put back in the wrong place. As the breaking or rotting of a string often happened, confusion resulted. This is why errors frequently occurred in ancient books and why checking and correcting errors was considered such an important job by ancient people. Inevitably, many errors remained uncorrected that still present problems to scholars.

Classical Works During the Period of the *Jian Ce*

Books made of bamboo strips were in use for about 1,700 years, from the Shang Dynasty to the Western Han and Eastern Han dynasties.

As we have said above, the Chinese written script developed during the late stages of primitive communal society. But as class society developed, creating a slave state, all written knowledge became the exclusive property of the ruling class. The rulers saw to it that their speeches and decisions were recorded by official historians. Included among these official historians were the diviners credited with interpreting the inscriptions on tortoise shells during the Shang Dynasty. And the inscribed writing on bronzewares was also done by the official historians of the time.

During the Shang and Zhou dynasties and the Spring and Autumn and Warring States periods, the dynastic rulers and vassal chiefs charged their official historians with the duty of collecting and keeping all official documents and government records. This was true up to the end of the Qing Dynasty. And from the beginning of the Shang Dynasty to the latter part of the Spring and Autumn Period the official historians were the only people who could read and write, since they had easy access to books. Underlining this is the saying recorded in history books that "all academic pursuits are placed under the exclusive control of the royal house". There were many books of that time whose authorship is attributed to the official historians. No writen works prior to the Spring and Autumn

Period, with the exception of the oracle bone and bronze inscriptions, have survived.

The oldest existing books are those edited or written by Confucius at the end of the Spring and Autumn Period. These include *Shi Jing* (*The Book of Songs*); *Shu Jing* (*The Book of Documents*); *Chun Qiu* (*The Spring and Autumn Annals*), based on the contemporary records of the State of Lu; *Yi Li* (*The Book of Rites*); *Yue Jing* (*The Book of Music*); and *Yi Jing* (*The Book of Changes*). Confucius taught his pupils from these six books, known to history as Six Classics of the Confucian School. He taught not only the sons of the nobility but also pupils from among the common people. This was the beginning of the dissemination of book knowledge among a wider section of the population, as against its monopoly by a privileged few members of the ruling class. Later, with annotation work done by such people as Dong Zhongshu (179-104 B.C.), the great textual research scholar and philosopher of the Western Han Dynasty, the Six Classics, together with Confucian teachings, began to function as the ideological and spiritual pillar of the feudal age. They became, in fact, the works most representative of the country's feudal culture.

In the period of the Warring States, the works of many great thinkers — Lao Zi, Zhuang Zi, Mo Zi, Shang Yang, Han Fei and others — became widely known. Though none of these authors aligned themselves with Confucius and his school, their works have enjoyed wide circulation over the past several thousand years, and they have exerted great influence in China's history. Among the proponents of the Confucian School were Zi Xia, Zi Si, Mencius and Xun Zi.

It was in this same period that Qu Yuan, the great

poet-patriot, wrote his immortal *Li Sao* (*The Lament*), *Jiu Ge* (*Nine Elegies*) and *Tian Wen* (*Heaven Asks*), books that have been handed down through the centuries as gems of Chinese literature. In military science there were works by Sun Wu, Sun Bin and Wu Qi, the most outstanding of which is the 13-*bian Sun Wu's Art of War. Sun Bin's Art of War*, considered lost for over 1,000 years, was finally brought to light in 1972 when it was unearthed in a tomb at Yingqueshan in Linyi, Shandong Province. *Huang Di Nei Jing* (*The Yellow Emperor's Classics of Internal Medicine*) and *Shen Nong Ben Cao Jing* (*Emperor Shen Nong's Materia Medica*) were the major medical works of that time. And in the field of astronomy there was *Xing Jing* (*The Star Manual*), while in mathematics there were *Zhou Bi* or *Zhou Bi Suan Jing* (*The Arithmetical Classic of the Gnomon and the Circular Paths*) and *Jiu Zhang Suan Shu* (*Nine Chapters on the Mathematical Art*). Books on philosophy, literature, general science, etc. flourished during this time, known in history as a time of all schools of thought contending for popularity.

In 221 B.C. the last of the warring states fell before the onslaught of Qin Shi Huang, the first emperor of the Qin Dynasty, and China was unified into an empire. In consolidating state power, he saw to it that a whole series of measures were enforced to ensure the unity of the country and strengthen his feudal rule. One of his policies to stamp out resistance was most brutal and obscurantist. He decreed the "burning of books" throughout the country, except for those dealing with the history of Qin, medicine, pharmacy, divination, agriculture and arboriculture.

Most ill-fated were the works of the Confucian School, such as *Shi Jing* and *Shu Jing*, and those belonging to the various schools of thought that flourished during pre-

Qin times. Any discussions of *Shi Jing* and *Shu Jing* were punishable by death, and those who criticized the present state of affairs by the pre-Qin standards were to be executed together with their families and kinsmen. Anyone who failed to turn in their books, as decreed, was to be branded on the face or forced to perform corvee service. More than 400 Confucian scholars were buried alive. This was the well-known "burning of books and burial of scholars alive" event, and it was the first unprecedented devastation brought upon Chinese books.

Because of the large-scale destruction, an enormous number of books of the Pre-Qin period perished. *Yue Jing*, for example, never reappeared, while *Shu Jing* and *Yi Li* are now incomplete. May other books are probably lost for ever.

It should be noted, however, that Qin Shi Huang only had the books owned by private individuals burned. The books kept in government custody remained intact, except for history books about states vanquished by the Qin. To the emperor, books could have no other purpose than to serve his rulership. But even the books that remained in Qin library failed to survive the conflagration of 206 B. C., when Xiang Yu* set Xianyang, capital of Qin, on fire and burnt it down.

It goes without saying that the "burning of books" decreed by Qin Shi Huang could never be complete. People hid books in various ways — in caves, in the walls of their homes, and in all manner of places. The order prohibiting the private possession of books was not rescinded until 191 B.C., the fourth year of the reign of Emperor Hui Di (194-187 B.C.). Some 50 years later, Emperor Wu

---

* Leader of one of the forces that rose against the Qin regime.

Di, under whose reign the country prospered, came to see the importance of books. He ordered the establishment of national libraries and engaged professional copists to make duplicate copies of books. This was the first recorded instance in Chinese history of the government officially collecting books and setting up national libraries. Under Emperor Wu Di's encouragement, many books were brought out of hiding. Since they were made of bamboo strips and had long been hidden underground, many of the strings were broken and the strips had become so disarranged that it was hard to make anything out of them. Nevertheless, books were now circulated and played a great role in preserving ancient culture.

A century later, in 26 B.C., Emperor Cheng Di ordered another collection of books for the national libraries. Officials were sent to different parts of the country to make inquiries and to collect books. Scholars, such as Liu Xiang (succeeded after his death by his son, Liu Xin); strategists, such as Ren Hong; medical men, such as Li Zhuguo; and astronomers, such as Yin Xian, were appointed to study and rearrange the bamboo strips. As a result, the first book catalogue in Chinese history — *Seven Categories of Writings* — was completed. This was later included by Ban Gu in his *History of the Han Dynasty*.

Having been re-examined and verified, ancient books were now kept in the national library of Tian Lu Ke. The pre-Qin books that survived Qin Shi Huang's destruction and the Xianyang fire have contributed a great deal to the development of China's culture. Later, many other books were lost in a fire at Chang'an, when Wang Mang and Liu Xiu were locked in struggle for the throne. During the Eastern Han Dynasty, the collection and re-editing of some books was also undertaken. But towards the end of that dynasty, again as a result of war, almost all the books so collected were lost.

But during the Eastern Han Dynasty three great events took place in the development of Chinese books. First, paper began to be used in making duplicate copies of books, thereby making it possible to have more books than before. Second, the process of making stone rubbings from the stone classics erected in the late years of the Eastern Han Dynasty pointed the way to the invention of printing at a later period. And third, bookshops were established, making it much easier to obtain books. The period of the Western Han and Eastern Han dynasties was, in a word, an epoch of dazzling brilliance and one with a profound influence on the development of Chinese books.

Though Emperor Wu Di was the first emperor to order the collection and preservation of books in libraries, he also ordered the "banning of all schools of thought other than that of Confucius and the respecting of Confucius". Thenceforth only the works of Confucius were esteemed as classics, while those of other schools were restricted in circulation. Thus people's thinking was bound within a limited scope set by the ruling class, and this retarded the development of feudal culture.

Many famous works were produced during this period of the Western and Eastern Han dynasties. Among these were the now lost laws and decrees formulated by Xiao He, regulations drawn up by Zhang Cang, military strategies put forward by Han Xin, and court rites prescribed by Shusun Tong that played a great role in strengthening the rule of the Western Han Dynasty. *Xin Yu* (*New Talks*) by Lu Jia, *Xin Shu* (*New Political Views*) by Jia Yi, *Huai Nan Zi* (*The Book of Huainan Zi*) by Liu An, *Chun Qiu*

Fan Lu (*Spring and Autumn Studies*) by Dong Zhongshu, and *Fa Yan* (a book modelled after *Analects of Confucius*) and *Tai Xuan Jing* (a book modelled after *The Book of Changes*) by Yang Xiong were major works produced on philosophy, copies of which still exist. Also of great importance is *Shi Ji* (*Records of the Historian*) by Sima Qian, which is not only a pioneering work in history but is also a well-known classic in literature. A classic dealing with agriculture from this period is *Fan Sheng Zhi Shu* (*The Book of Fan Shengzhi*). There were also the writers Sima Xiangru, Mei Chen and Dongfang Shuo, whose writings of poetic prose and writings of descriptive prose interspersed with verse were works particularly representative of Western Han times.

Prominent among the works of the Eastern Han Dynasty was the materialist and philosophical work *Lun Heng* (*Discourses Weighed in the Balance*) by the great thinker Wang Chong. Besides this, there was the major dynastic history *Han Shu* (*History of the Han Dynasty*) presented as a series of biographies by Ban Gu. This became a model for succeeding historians. *Shuo Wen Jie Zi* (*Analytical Dictionary of Characters*) by Xu Shen was the earliest philological work in China to make a systematic study of words. *Shang Han Lun* (*A Treatise on Fevers*) by Zhang Zhongjing and the theory that the sky was like an eggshell and the earth like a yolk by Zhang Heng remain landmarks in the development of ancient medical science and astronomy.

Towards the end of the Eastern Han Dynasty, polemic writings by the critics Wang Fu, Ying Shao, Cui Shi, Xu Gan and Zhong Changtong provided models for the later philosophical works of the Wei and Jin dynasties. Poems and songs by the "seven talents of Jianan" (Jianan

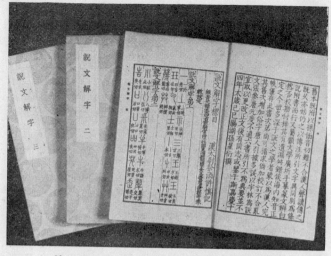

Shuo Wen Jie Zi (Analytical Dictionary of Characters), one of the world's oldest dictionaries

was the reign title of Emperor Xian Di during the closing years of the Eastern Han), Wang Can, Liu Zhen, Kong Rong, Chen Lin, Xu Gan, Ruan Yu and Ying Yang, demonstrated the great achievements of literature during this dynasty. The later years of the Eastern Han Dynasty also saw Buddhist scriptures being translated into Chinese, Through these translations, foreign ideas first entered China in a systematic way to be gradually incorporated into the culture of the people.

It should be pointed out that the school of Confucianism also developed in this period. Books annotating the remaining Five Classics of Confucianism, after the destruction of the *Yue Jing (The Book of Music)*, included the *Shang Shu Da Zhuan (Great Commentary on "The Book of History")* by Fu Sheng, *Shi Xun Gu (Exegetics of*

Poetry) by Mao Gong, *Han Shi Wai Zhuan* (*Anecdotes on "The Book of Songs"*) by Han Ying, *Chun Qiu Gong Yang Zhuan* (*Gong Yang's Commentary on "The Spring and Autumn Annals"*) and *Chun Qiu Gu Liang Zhuan* (*Gu Liang's Commentary on "The Spring and Autumn Annals"*). The *Yi Jing* (*The Book of Changes*), *Li Yi* (*Records of Rites*), *Zhou Li* (*Rites of the Zhou Dynasty*), *Chun Qiu Zuo Shi Zhuan* (*Zuo Qiuming's Commentary on "The Spring and Autumn Annals"*) and *Er Ya* (*Literary Expositor*) also became available at this time. And there were many exegetic works, including the Five Classics with annotations by Zheng Xuan, *Gong Yang's Commentary on "The Spring and Autumn Annals"* with an exegesis by He Xiu and *Zuo Qiuming's Commentary on "The Spring and Autumn Annals"* elaborated by Jia Kui and Fu Qian. But books like these have all been lost. As to those works that survived, they offer us the best material for studying Confucian classics and the laws, decrees and cultural affairs of the Qin and Han dynasties. Research related to these classics has been known throughout history as "Han-style learning or learning in the style of the Han Dynasty scholars", a fact that points to the great influence of the Western Han and Eastern Han classics on people of succeeding generations.

In summary, the time when books made of bamboo strips were in use was a time when the culture of feudal society developed and classical works in philosophy, literature, science, etc. began to appear. Of course, during the Warring States Period books also appeared that were made of silk fabrics, and by the Eastern Han Dynasty there were books made of paper. But books made of bamboo strips were the general rule, and they extended over a long period of Chinese history. The feudal rulers, for the first time, ordered the collection and re-editing of books. At the same time they suppressed many books. And because of wars and fire, a large number of important books were lost.

Chapter IV

Writings on Silk and Books Made of Scrolls and Rods

Writings on Silk Fabrics

The Warring States Period saw two great developments in the production of Chinese books. The first was the birth of many unofficial writers, as the system of emperors employing official historians disintegrated. The other was the appearance of writings on silk that eventually led to the invention of paper and the subsequent changes in the system of book making.

It was approximately during the intervening time between the Spring and Autumn Period and the Warring States Period that writing on silk fabrics first appeared. At this time bamboo strips and wooden slats were still used extensively for book making. Silk fabrics were called *bo* (帛) or *jian* (缣) at this time. A book made of silk fabrics was called a *bo shu* (帛书) or *jian shu* (缣书), meaning a silk book. Mo Zi, a philosopher of the 4th century B.C., is quoted as saying: "Write on bamboo or silk, engrave on metal or stone." This shows that in Mo Zi's time silk was already used side by side with bamboo and wood as a material for book making.

It is reasonable to assume that silk was used to make books because of the unsatisfactory nature of the bamboo strips. Silk is soft and light. It could be folded or rolled up, and it was easy to carry or store. It was also more useful for books that had illustrations than was bamboo or wood, because the shape of a piece of cloth was more variable.

Silk could be cut to the exact length needed for each piece of writing; and it could then be folded. Thus silk books had no fixed size, their length depending on their subject matter. Although the silk could be folded, records show it was usually rolled. One roll, or scroll (*juan*), was equivalent to a bundle (*bian*) of bamboo strips. Each *juan* contained a complete essay or a number of short articles, since a short piece of silk containing only one short article could not be easily rolled. *Juan* thus became the designation for a fascicle of a book as well as a chapter in a book.

Silk scroll books originated approximately at the end of the Spring and Autumn Period, gradually became prevalent in the early Warring States Period, and continued to be used through the Qin and Han dynasties. In a catalogue of the national library in the *History of the Han Dynasty*, a fascicle or a chapter was called either *bian* or *juan*, or both. *Bian* was used for a bundle or bundles of bamboo strips and *juan* for a silk scroll or scrolls. This testifies to the fact that during the western Han Dynasty, books made of bamboo strips and wooden slats existed side by side with books made of silk fabrics. The fact that the word *juan* appeared less often than *bian* shows that silk for books was less often used. Though paper had been invented by the time of the Eastern Han Dynasty, it was still not used very much in book making.

During the civil disturbances of the latter part of the Eastern Han Dynasty, silk books were appropriated for military use. They were turned into tents, chariot covers and bags or satchels. This suggests that there were a surprising number of silk scrolls available at that time. Following the Three Kingdoms Period (220-280) there was a gradual replacement of bamboo and silk by paper. By the Western and Eastern Jin dynasties (265-420) and the Southern and Northern Dynasties (420-589) silk books were seldom seen. Only the wealthiest aristocrats could afford to use silk for writing letters. Paper, however, was popularly used. The period of silk-scroll books lasted about 600 or 700 years, down to the 3rd century.

Remains of silk scrolls were unearthed from a site near Loulan, in Xinjiang, before Liberation. In 1951 silk scrolls were also found in a tomb near Changsha that belonged to the Kingdom of Chu in the Warring States Period. But in both cases, these books contained only the remains of religious pictures and some annotations. Most of the silk had rotted underground over the centuries, leaving only shreds.

Complete silk books were unearthed in 1973. They were found in the Mawangdui tomb of Changsha, in Hunan Province, which dates back to the 12th year (168 B.C.) of the Qianyuan reign of Emperor Wen Di of the Han Dynasty. Among the books in the tomb were two lost editions of *The Book of Lao Zi*, respectively named Edition A and Edition B; *The Book of Changes*; *Zhan Guo Ce* (*Sayings of the Warring States*); *Zuo Qiuming's Commentary on "The Spring and Autumn Annals"*; *Tian Wen Zhan Xing* (*Astronomical Astrology*); *Yi Jing* (*Classic on Medicine*), and *Xiang Ma Jing* (*Horse Manual*), more than 20 titles totalling 100,000 characters. At the end of Edition A and the beginning of Edition B of *The Book of Lao Zi* are four articles not included in existing editions of the book. Edition A contains 463 lines of more than 13,000

characters; Edition B has 252 lines of over 16,000 characters. According to the archeologists, the former was copied in the years from 206-195 B.C., during the reign of Emperor Gao Zu of the Han Dynasty, while the latter was done approximately in the years 194 to 180 B.C. during the reign of Emperor Hui Di of the Han Dynasty. They were found in a pile at the bottom of a rectangular mirror box. Interestingly enough, these were not *juan*, which shows our ancient silk books were sometimes not rolled as scrolls.

A part of the *Zhan Guo Ce* (*Saying of the Warring States*), unearthed from a Han tomb

Found among the burial objects in this tomb were also three ancient tri-coloured silk maps, showing mountains, rivers, cities, towns, and even streets. Of the three, the most noteworthy is a military map. This highlights the deployment of military forces and commanding fortifications. The defence areas are clearly delineated. Finely executed and produced with great accuracy, the map points to ancient achievements in cartography and the scientific level of geographical surveys in China at that time. As the oldest maps so far discovered, these three offer important data for making studies of military science in the Western Han Dynasty.

Silk was expensive. In fact there was a saying during the Eastern Han Dynasty: "It's not so convenient to use silk because it is dear." It was impossible for the common people to be able to afford silk for writing. A substance had to be found which, retaining the advantages of silk, would be cheaper. That substance was paper.

The Invention of Paper

Because bamboo strips and wooden slats were bulky and silk was expensive, these materials placed limits on the expansion of book making. Paper had the advantage of being easy to write on, being easy to store and carry around, and being cheap as well. With its use, marvelous feats were achieved and knowledge propagated. Thus the invention of paper constituted a most significant event in history. The credit for this invention goes to the Chinese.

Fan Ye, who lived in the 5th century, wrote a biography of the so-called originator of paper, Cai Lun,

Cai Lun (?-121)

in the *Hou Han Shu* (*History of the Later Han Dynasty*).
Fan Ye wrote:

> In ancient times, books were largely made of
> bamboo strips; some were made of silk, a material
> that was called *zhi* (paper). As bamboo strips were
> bulky and silk expensive, books made of such mate-
> rials were not handy. Cai Lun suggested using tree
> bark, hemp, rags, or old fishing nets to make paper.
> In the first year of Yuan Xing [A.D. 105] of Em-
> peror He Di of the Eastern Han Dynasty, he re-
> ported this invention to the emperor, who commended
> him for his ingenuity. From that time on, paper came
> to be widely used.

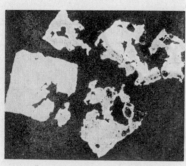

Paper made from hemp,
Western Han Dynasty

According to Fan
Ye, Cai Lun lived
during the Eastern
Han Dynasty, and in-
vented paper in A.D.
105.

Historical rec-
ords, however, show
that paper had al-
ready come into use
in China before A.D.
105. Xu Sheng, a
contemporary of Cai Lun, told of the process of paper
making in his dictionary, the earliest in China, called
Shuo Wen Jie Zi (*Analytical Dictionary of Characters*) and
completed about A.D. 100. Xu Sheng gave a substantial
description of the process of paper making at that time.
He said that paper was made by putting silk waste in
water and beating it into a thick fluid. The fluid was

then spread over a fine bamboo screen, and when it was dry, paper sheets were formed.

Further evidence of the fact that paper was made at this early date is a statement in the *History of the Han Dynasty,* "Chapter on the Life of Zhao Feiyan" where it says that in the year 12 B.C., during the reign of Emperor Cheng Di of the Western Han, paper made of silk waste was already used for wrapping medicines at the Imperial Court. When Jia Kui was asked to teach his students *Zuo Qiuming's Commentary on "The Spring and Autumn Annals",* he gave his students "two classics" to read, "one made of paper and the other made of bamboo strips", according to the *History of the Later Han Dynasty,* "Chapter on the Life of Jia Kui". That was in the year A.D. 76, this book says. Evidently the paper used was made of silk waste.

Since tree bark, hemp ends, etc. were used by Cai Lun in making paper, this was a great technical improvement over the use of silk waste, making mass production of paper possible. But this still cannot be called an original invention, or an invention only to Cai Lun's credit. Other evidence is available to us that shows that paper had already been made with fibre plants before Cai Lun's time.

In 1933, at the site of an ancient fortress in Lop Nur, Xinjiang, a piece of paper was found that was made of hemp. Investigation showed that the paper was of a primitive type, as judged by its poor quality and the fact that its fibres were still discernible on the paper surface. Among some of the other things found with this piece of old paper were some wooden slats that dated back to the first year (49 B.C.) of the Huang Long reign of the Western Han Emperor Xuan Di. The paper thus came from the time of the Western Han Dynasty.

In 1957, several pieces of paper were found in an old tomb on the worksite of the Baqiao Brick and Tile Factory in Xi'an. They dated back to the first or second century B.C., during the reign of Emperor Wu Di. Analysis by electronic microscope showed that the paper was made of hemp fibres. This also shows that by the Western Han Dynasty people had known how to make paper out of hemp fibres, even though they had not yet used the paper for writing. During the Western Han Dynasty the paper was used exclusively for wrapping (that unearthed at the Baqiao site was used for wrapping a bronze mirror) because of its poor quality. Yet it is clear that paper made of fibre plants had existed for about 100 years before Cai Lun was officially credited with inventing the paper-making technique.

In 1974, paper with characters written on it was found in the excavation of an old tomb at Wuwei, Gansu Province. This paper dated back to the time of the Eastern Han Dynasty. The paper, called Hantanpo Paper after the worksite where the tomb was found, was made of bast fibres. It was of much better quality than the Baqiao Paper unearthed at Xi'an, which shows that the paper-making techniques had advanced.

What, then, can be said about Cai Lun's contribution to paper making? Cai Lun was a eunuch at the imperial household of the Eastern Han Dynasty. Since he was the court official in charge of the imperial household necessities, he probably had contact with people who made primitive forms of paper as well as the best craftsmen in paper making from all over the country. This enabled him to perfect and publicize the paper-making process then in use. Probably he merely reported to the emperor what he knew about the invention. Only through such reports would the inventions of labouring people in feudal society become known to the rulers of that time. Thus the invention of paper should really be attributed to the efforts of the labouring people over a long period of time, and Cai Lun merely played a part in perfecting and publicizing the process.

Paper composed of fibre plants could be made cheaply, and so mass production was possible. In time, better-quality papers were made of a great variety of materials, including the bark of mulberry trees, the bark of sandal-wood trees, etc. Rattan was exploited for paper making during the Jin Dynasty according to written records that say the paper was used for writing. During the Tang Dynasty, bast-fibre plants were still the main material used for paper making. In the Song Dynasty (960-1279) bamboo was used, and this was increasingly the case in the succeeding Yuan (1279-1368) and Ming (1368-1644) dynasties. Thereafter, a mixture of materials were used to make paper, depending on the type of paper desired. The materials included wheat stalks and straw.

It was much more difficult to make paper with tree bark or bamboo than with bast-fibre plants, which shows that the techniques of paper making had progressed. An episode in Honoré de Balzac's *Illusions perdues* illustrates the high opinion in which China's paper making was held by Europeans. Balzac tells of two erudite proofreaders who made a bet on a piece of paper from China. One said that it was made of fibre plants while the other held that it was made of some sort of animal material, probably silk cocoons. They consulted an expert who specialized in paper, and this person expressed the opinion that paper in China was made only with bamboo pulp. Though the three failed to resolve the dispute, their words underline

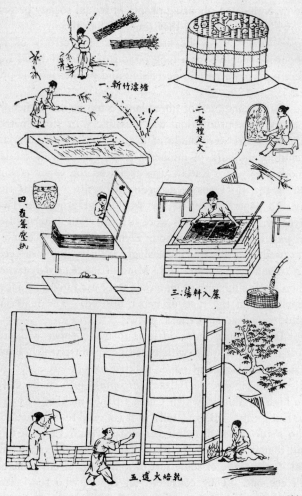

一、斬竹漂塘

二、煮楻足火

三、蕩料入簾

四、覆簾壓紙

五、透火焙乾

Schematic diagram showing the art of paper making in ancient China

the fact that China's high standards of paper making were well-known throughout the world.

History records that the year 751 saw the first spread of Chinese paper making outside the country. That year some soldiers of the Tang Dynasty were taken captive in a war with Arabia. These soldiers took the technique of paper making to the Arab world. Paper mills were soon set up in Samarkand, and so the Arabs were the first people to manufacture paper beyond the borders of China. Following this, paper mills were set up in Baghdad in 793, in Egypt in 900 and in Morocco in 1100. In 1150, the first European paper factory was opened in Spain. After that, paper mills were set up one after another in other European countries. The first paper mill set up in America was in Philadelphia in 1690.

Paper making was introduced into the Orient at a much earlier date. It was introduced into Korea and Viet Nam about the middle of the 3rd century, and into Japan from Korea in the 5th century. India learned how to make paper by the overland route from China in the 6th century. As the art spread, the wisdom and labour of other peoples contributed to raising the standards of paper making throughout the world.

The Scroll and Rod System

Though paper first appeared in China in the 2nd century B.C., its use for writing in place of bamboo strips, wooden slats or silk fabrics occurred much later. Thus there was a period of time in which bamboo, silk and paper were simultaneously used for writing. The gradual substitution of paper for bamboo, wood and silk took place

51

only in A.D. 404 when Huan Xuan issued an order banning the use of bamboo strips and wooden slats.

We have not yet discovered any book made of paper that dates back to the century in which paper first came into use for writing. From the archeological finds of the last few years we have learned, however, that the earliest paper books were in the form of scrolls. Part of the work *San Guo Zhi* (*History of the Three Kingdoms*) was unearthed in 1924 in Shanshan County, Xinjiang. It dates back to the Jin Dynasty, and has 80 lines totalling more than 1,000 characters. Because it was taken abroad, only a photostat copy remains in China. In January 1965, at the site of a Buddhist pagoda in Turpan, Xinjiang, another part of the *History of the Three Kingdoms* was discovered by archeologists. This section, also dating back to the Jin period, contained "The Life of Sun Quan" in 40 lines totalling more than 500 characters. Done in neat *li* (official) script, these two remnants of the *History of the Three Kingdoms* date back to the 4th century, not long after the completion of the original work by Chen Shou.

Among other archeological finds are some paper scrolls from the 5th century as well as the 7th to the 9th centuries. Particularly noteworthy are the first five chapters of *Lun Yu Zheng Shi Zhu* (*Analects of Confucius with Annotation by Zheng Xuan*) unearthed from an old tomb in Turpan, Xinjiang, and dating back to the Tang Dynasty. Though incomplete, at the end of the chapter of *Gongye Chang* is the clear signature of a young copist: "Bo Tianshou, a pupil, on February 1, in the 4th year of the Jinglong reign." The inscription includes his age, 12, his birthplace and a few lines of his random thoughts. Since the 4th year of the Jinglong reign was the last year Emperor Zhong

Fragment of the manuscript of the *Analects of Confucius* with annotations by Zheng Xuan, Tang Dynasty

Zong was on the throne, the year when the young calligrapher completed this work was 710. The scroll fragments give witness to the universal practice of copying books during the Tang Dynasty.

Large numbers of paper scrolls, dating from the 5th to the 9th centuries, have been found in good condition in the Thousand-Buddha Caves at Dunhuang, Gansu Province. We know from this that the form of the earliest paper books followed that of silk scrolls. Sheets of paper were pasted together and rolled sidewise around a rod to form the scroll. This was called the scroll and rod system. The ancients also invented a colouring process to protect the paper. The "yellow paper" thus produced was dyed with an extract from the bark of a cork tree — a treatment that protected it against insect pests. The length of each paper scroll depended on the length of the subject, while the scroll width was usually about one foot. On the paper,

53

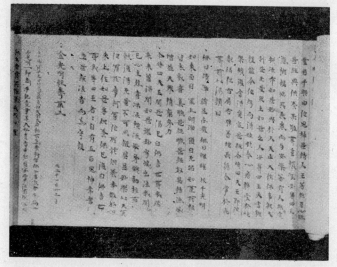

Scroll and rod: fragment of the hand-copied *Suvarna-prabbasottama Sutra*, Eastern Jin Dynasty

ruled columns, called the "borders", were drawn. The upper and lower "borders" were called the "edges".

The rod was usually a tiny, painted wooden stick, as were the ones unearthed at Dunhuang. Rods were sometimes also made of other materials — glazed porcelain, ivory, coral, red sandalwood, and even jade or gold for scrolls owned by the imperial household or the nobility.

To protect a scroll from damage, it was mounted on a piece of paper or silk fabric called *biao* (褾). A cord for tying the scroll was attached to the *biao*. Much attention was paid to this cord, which might be in any one of a number of different colours and specially woven.

A book often contained many scrolls. Some method, therefore, had to be devised to avoid confusion. A piece of cloth or other material was used to wrap together all the scrolls which made up a book. One wrapper, or "book clothes", usually contained five to 10 scrolls. And a book of considerable length would require more than one wrap-

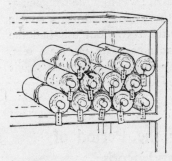

per. The wrapper itself was made of silk or hemp. Some ancient wrappers were made of fine bamboo threads crosswoven with silk. These were called "bamboo wrappers". A string at one end of the wrapper was used to tie the scrolls together. When placed on a shelf, the ends of the scrolls could then be

Scrolls on shelf with tags

seen. A tag, marked with the name of the book, number of the scroll or other particulars, was attached to each scroll so that it could be easily picked out of, or put back into, the wrapper.

In writing, the first two columns were often left for the title of the essay or chapter heading and the number of the scroll. A few spaces were also reserved for the title of the book (the main title). At the end of the text, a column was reserved for the date of the copying and the name of the copyist (this column is blank in many ancient scrolls), and another for listing of the title of the essay or chapter and the number of the scroll. Sometimes a few more columns contained comments on the work by the copyist. That was the origin for the practice of writing a postscript at the end of a book.

No restriction was set on the number of characters in

each column in ancient scrolls. But usually it had 20 to a dozen characters per column. The customary practice between the 3rd and the 6th centuries was that, if a book was annotated, the text was written in red ink and the annotation in black. Another practice was to write the annotation in smaller characters within one column or in double columns immediately below the text. But this had the disadvantage of confusing the notes with the main text. This is one reason why many ancient hand-copied scrolls are so difficult to read and understand.

Works During the Period of Scrolls and Rods

Books in scroll form were in use from the 2nd to the 10th centuries, and they were all copied by hand. As paper became more readily available, the number of copyists increased. During the Tang Dynasty there were many professional copyists, and bookshops also increased. Consequently, there were many more works produced in this period that have been preserved than there were in earlier periods. The writers of the Eastern Han Dynasty and after flourished in the field of history. Their books included the *History of the Three Kingdoms* by Chen Shou and the *History of the Later Han Dynasty* by Fan Ye, both well-known works of dynastic history, or "historical records" presented as a series of biographies.

The *Wei Shu* (*History of the Wei Dynasty*) by Wei Shou of Northern Qi (550-557), Song Shu (*History of the Song Dynasty*) by Shen Yue of Liang (502-557), and *Nan Qi Shu* (*History of the Southern Qi Dynasty*) by Xiao

Zixian are also examples of history books written in biographical style. By instituting a bureau of history during the Tang Dynasty, Emperor Tai Zong saw to it that *Jin Shu* (*History of the Jin Dynasty*), *Bei Qi Shu* (*History of the Northern Qi Dynasty*), *Zhou Shu* (*History of the Northern Zhou Dynasty*), *Liang Shu* (*History of the Liang Dynasty*), *Chen Shu* (*History of the Chen Dynasty*) and *Sui Shu* (*History of the Sui Dynasty*) were compiled. These histories were models for later official history books. At the same time, there was a gradual prohibition of history books being written about previous dynasties. Yet there were some books during the Tang Dynasty, such as *Nan Shi* (*History of the Southern Dynasties*) and *Bei Shi* (*History of the Northern Dynasties*) by Li Yanshou, that had received official endorsement. Alongside these were a number of annals of history biographies, and works dealing with geography that featured the customs and local produce in various places. As a result, books such as *Shi Tong* (*Critique of Historical Works*) by Liu Zhiji of Tang were written. These catalogued the books related to history and were pioneering studies in historiography.

Before the Three Kingdoms Period, all literary works were single pieces. Collections of works didn't appear until the end of the Eastern Han Dynasty. Selections then followed, giving people easy access to an ever increasing number of works by different authors. *Wen Zhang Liu Bie Zhi* (*Classified Anthology*) by Zhi Yu of the Western Jin Dynasty is said to be the earliest of these. (*The Book of Songs* and *Elegies of Chu* are actually the oldest, but they have been lost.) *Wen Xuan* (*Anthology Through the Ages*) by Xiao Tong, apparent to Emperor Wu Di of the Liang Dynasty, was a work that exerted an enormous influence at that time. *Yu Tai Xin Yong* (*New Verses of Jade Ter-*

race) by Xu Ling of the Chen Dynasty (557-589) was another famous anthology.

Literary criticism also developed during this period. *Dian Lun* (*Historical Allusions and Essays*) by Cao Pi, *Wen Fu* (*On Poetry Writing*) by Lu Ji of Western Jin, *Wen Xin Diao Long* (*Carving a Dragon at the Core of Literature*) by Liu Xie of the Liang Dynasty and *Shi Ping* (*Critique of Poetry*) by Zhong Rong were important works in the history of literary criticism, and they represented a new field of interest.

In the same period there appeared reference books. These were much needed because readers were presented with no small difficulties by the prodigious number of works that were now in circulation. With the material from various sources categorically arranged into different subjects in these reference books, users gained access to a wide range of works by ancient authors. *Huang Lan* (*Imperial Encyclopedia*), compiled under the orders of Cao Pi, Emperor Wen Di of the Wei Dynasty, is known as the earliest work serving this purpose. Another famous work was *Xiu Wen Dian Yu Lan* (*Xiuwen Hall Imperial Encyclopedia*) by Zu Xiaozheng and others of the Northern Qi Dynasty. Included among these was also the *Wen Si Bo Yao* (*Selections of Miscellaneous Writings*), totalling 1,200 fascicles, that was compiled by Xu Jingzong and others under the orders of Emperor Tai Zong of the Tang Dynasty, and *San Jiao Zhu Ying* (*Choice Selections of Miscellaneous Writings*), totalling 1,300 fascicles, that was compiled by Zhang Changzong and others under the orders of Empress Wu Zetian (627-705). But these compilations have not survived to the present day. Among the reference books that no longer survive are also a number of works compiled by individuals during the period of the Six

Dynasties (3rd-6th centuries), some comprising a few dozen fascicles and one comprising several hundred.

During the Tang Dynasty reference books compiled by individuals became more common. Fine material for research into the history of pre-Tang dynasties was provided by these reference books, copies of which still exist: *Yi Wen Lei Ju* (*Literary Records Collected and Classified*) by Ouyang Xun, *Bei Tang Shu Chao* (*Book Records of the Northern Hall*) by Yu Shinan, *Chu Xue Ji* (*The Primary Anthology*) by Xu Jian and *Liu Tie* (*Six Cards*) by Bai Juyi.

Translations of Buddhist scriptures into Chinese also provided books beginning in the late Eastern Han Dynasty. Dharmaraksa of the Western Jin Dynasty, Kumarajiva (344-413) of the Later Qin Dynasty (384-417), Gunabhadra (394-468) of the Song Dynasty and Xuan Zang of the Tang Dynasty were among the best translators of Buddhist scriptures, and Xuan Zang was the most outstanding.

At this time there were also a number of studies of Buddhist scriptures written. Catalogues recording Buddhist works were first written in the Wei and Jin dynasties. During the reign of Emperor Xuan Zong of the Tang Dynasty, Monk Zhi Sheng classified his own translations of Buddhist works and those of other Chinese authors under the title *Kai Yuan Shi Jiao Lu* (*The Kaiyuan Catalogue of Buddhist Works*). This served as the foundation for the collection of Buddhist scriptures, *Tripitaka* in Chinese, that totalled 5,040 fascicles. In subsequent years additions and reductions were made to this work, but it has always remained in size at around 5,000 to 6,000 fascicles.

By the late Eastern Han Dynasty copies of Taoist

classics also appeared. The *Taoist Patrology* was compiled under the orders of Emperor Xuan Zong of the Tang Dynasty. It totalled 3,744 fascicles, and was entitled *San Dong Qiong Gang* (*Collectanea from the Three Collections that Penetrate the Mystery*).

Because of the stress given to phonetics in the translation of Buddhist scriptures, there was great interest in phonology. Studies to that end had been undertaken by people like Li Deng as early as the Wei Dynasty (220-265). In time, people came to accept what is now known as the traditional method of indicating the pronunciation of a Chinese character, that is, by using two other Chinese characters, the first having the same consonant as the given character and the second having the same vowel (with or without final nasal) and tone, and the four tones of classical Chinese phonetics. This paved the way for modern semantics.

Many famous philosophical works were produced during this period. The doctrines of Lao Zi and Zhuang Zi were spread far and wide during the Wei and Jin dynasties. Works making an elaborate study of these doctrines were also put out in prodigious number. *Lao Zi Zhu* (*Annotations to "The Book of Lao Zi"*) by Wang Bi of the Wei Dynasty and *Zhuang Zi Zhu* (*Annotations to "The Book of Zhuang Zi"*) by Guo Xiang of the Jin Dynasty exerted particularly great influence. The materialist stand that refuted the religious and superstitious ideas prevalent at the time was put forward in *Wu Gui Lun* (*On the Non-existence of Ghosts*) by Ruan Zhan of the Jin Dynasty and *Shen Mie Lun* (*On the Destructibility of the Soul*) by Fan Zhen of the Liang Dynasty. These two works were of great importance in the country's philosophical history, though they were not generally accepted by people of the time.

It goes without saying that the ruling ideology throughout this period was that of the Confucian School, as taught in the national academies. New theses and ideas were found to explain the Confucian classics so that these writings were not just a repetition of the ideas popularized during the Han Dynasty. For examples, during the Wei Dynasty, Wang Su made a point of refuting the Confucian commentaries of Zheng Xuan in his annotations to the Five Classics. A thorough refutation of the superstitious concepts that originated in the Han Dynasty was given by Wang Bi in his *Yi Zhu* (*Commentary on "The Book of Changes"*) and *Yi Lue Li* (*Brief Exposition of "The Book of Changes"*). Many new explanations and ideas were also found in He Yan's *Lun Yu Ji Jie* (*Commentary on "Analects of Confucius"*). Such works during the Tang Dynasty included Kong Yingda's *Wu Jing Zheng Yi* (*Annotations to the Five Classics*) and Jia Gongyan's commentaries on *The Book of Rites* and *Rites of the Zhou Dynasty*. The latter two became part of the noted work *Shi San Jing Zhu Shu* (*Thirteen Classics with Collected Commentaries*).

As to the other philosophical schools that existed before the Qin Dynasty, many had passed out of existence after the enforcement of the Han emperor Wu Di's order to ban propagation of all non-Confucian ideas.

Particularly noticeable during this period was the appearance of works in science and technology, as represented by the writings of Zu Chongzhi in mathematics and Jia Sixie's *Qi Min Yao Shu* (*The Manual of Important Arts for the People*).

During the Southern and Northern Dynasties and the

Sui and Tang dynasties, an increasing number of books were produced, and large collections of books were made by the government and individuals. Emperor Yuan Di (552-554) of the Liang Dynasty collected more than 67,000 *juan* of hand-copied books. Emperor Yang Di (605-618) of the Sui Dynasty ordered the hand-copying of more than 89,000 *juan* at Luoyang. Emperor Wen Zong (826-840) of the Tang Dynasty had 56,000 *juan* copied and kept at Chang'an. These books were beautifully bound, had jade rods, ivory tags, silken cords, and mounts in different colours to identify the specific classification for each *juan*. Private owners, such as Zhang Hua of the Western Jin Dynasty, Shen Yue and Ren Fang of the Liang Dynasty and Su Bian, Li Bi and Liu Gongchuo of the Tang Dynasty, each had from 20,000 to 30,000 hand-copied *juan* in their private libraries. As there were many Buddhists, hand-copying of Buddhist scriptures flourished in the monasteries from the Later Wei Dynasty (386-557) through the Sui and Tang dynasties. The Sui and Tang dynasties were the golden age of hand-copied books. Unfortunately, the greater part of these books were destroyed in subsequent wars.

An accidental discovery in the Thousand-Buddha Caves at Dunhuang, Gansu Province, in 1899, brought to light a large number of scrolls belonging to the period between the 5th and 10th centuries. These had been stored to protect them from the ravages of war. The discoverer, a Taoist priest named Wang, accidentally struck a sealed chamber in which he found piles of ancient scrolls. He did not know their value, and was tricked into giving the largest portion of them to an Englishman, Aurel Stein, and a Frenchman, Paul Pelliot. These two men took them to

Britain and France. Later, a few bureaucrat-scholars got away with a great many more of these ancient treasures. The remainder, about 8,000 scrolls, was sent to Beijing in 1909 where it was placed by the Manchu government in the Metropolitan Library at Beijing (now Beijing Library). This collection, together with later additions, amounts to 10,000 *juan*.

Among the finds at Dunhuang were some of the first printed books, paintings, woodcuts, brocades, embroideries and rubbings, but hand-copied scrolls formed the greatest part of the treasure. Among the hand-copied scrolls were Buddhist scriptures, Taoist scriptures, Confucian classics, books on philology and geography, medical books, novels, popular ballads, and books of divination. There were also poems, ballads, short essays, letters, account records, calendars, census records, contracts, official documents and oracles. They were in many languages including Han (being that predominantly used), Tangut, Tibetan, Sanskrit and various Central Asian languages, such as Kharoshthi, Sogdian, Khotanese, Uygur and Kuchean.

Nobody has yet been able to assess the exact amount of the material discovered. But the hand-copied scrolls are estimated to have included no less than 25,000 *juan*. Among them were the earliest hand-copied books dating back to the 5th century. The novels, ballads, folklore, *bian wen* (a kind of prose interspersed with verses) and so on had no precedents. Through them we have come to know what kind of literature the people of these ancient times were interested in. We have also profited by much newly discovered material on the history of Chinese literature. This has helped us correct errors and omissions in many printed books.

From Scrolls to Leaves

The period of the Sui and Tang dynasties, when hand copying flourished, was also the period when the scroll and rod system reached its height and when beautiful bindings appeared. In the mid-9th century, however, books in scroll form were gradually replaced by books in leaf form.

The scrolls were long — often several tens of feet — and rather troublesome to unroll. The process of looking up a single sentence in the text might require the unrolling of most of a scroll. During the Warring States Period and the Qin and Han dynasties scrolls caused few problems because there were few lengthy writings. But from the Sui and Tang dynasties onward, after a number of dictionaries had been published, the matter of looking up a word or a sentence was an oft-occurring necessity. The great inconvenience and inefficiency of rolling and unrolling became more and more of a problem.

Some inventive person then decided that, instead of using the scroll form, a book might be made by folding the paper to form a pile in a rectangular shape. The front and back covers of such a book were made of strong, thick paper, sometimes dyed in colour or mounted on cloth for protection. This new form was called a "leaf binding", or "sutra binding". With this new kind of binding, a reader could easily turn to any leaf to look up a word or a sentence, without having to unroll the whole book.

This was a great step forward in the development of books. Before long, however, this new form was also found to have some drawbacks. A long piece of folded paper could easily become unfolded and spread out. To avoid this, book makers added another sheet of paper to the folded pile. This was creased in the middle and one half

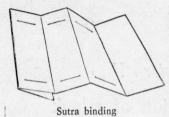

Sutra binding

of the sheet was pasted onto the first leaf and the other half was pasted onto the last leaf. The extra sheet held the pile together and prevented it from spreading out, while the leaves of the pile could still be turned forwards and backwards. This came to be called a "whirlwind binding".

These two forms of binding appeared in the mid-9th century. They overcame the defects of the scroll and rod system, yet they had a disadvantage in the fact that the place where the paper was folded might break after a lapse of time. Disarrangement and loss of leaves then occurred unavoidably. The next step was to bind the separate sheets into a book. When this step was taken books bound as they are today were created.

Whirlwind binding

Chapter V

The Invention of Block Printing and Its Development

The Invention of Block Printing

All books were copied by hand before the 9th century. If a hundred copies were needed, the text had to be written a hundred times. In the case of a voluminous work, the copying might take a dozen years to complete. Books therefore circulated very slowly and were difficult to obtain. At the same time, the limited number of duplicate copies made their loss through fire and war a severe problem. The knowledge they contained was too easily lost. As a result, the spread of knowledge was extremely slow.

The invention of printing, however, did away with this handicap. As soon as the printing blocks were carved, as many copies as needed could be produced. Reading thus became more convenient, and more people began to keep books. Greater interest was also aroused in writing books so that there was a speedy development of culture.

Everyone agrees that the art of printing, both by woodblocks and movable type, was invented by the Chinese people. But when was block printing invented? Opinions on this vary. Some hold that it was invented in the Sui Dynasty; others, in the Tang Dynasty; and still others, during the Five Dynasties (907-960).

The last view has been disproved by the fact that books printed in the 9th century have been discovered. The Sui Dynasty claim is also untenable, since it is based on a misinterpretation of existing documents. Scholars today generally agree that the art of printing was invented during the Tang Dynasty (618-907). This view is substantiated not only by documentary records, but also by printed books from that time.

Yet we are still left with the question: in what period of the 300-year-long Tang Dynasty did printing begin? Investigation of Tang printed matter and an examination of the records provides the answer.

The oldest printed materials, authenticated as to dates, are the *Diamond Sutra* (A. D. 868) and the calendars of 877 and 882. They were among the thousands of manuscripts discovered in Dunhuang and carried away to London by Aurel Stein. These show that printing was already being utilized in China as early as the latter part of the 9th century.

The *Diamond Sutra* is a scroll 14 Chinese feet long. It is complete in every detail, with a statement at the end saying that it was cut on the 15th day of the 4th moon of the 9th year of Xian Tong (A. D. 868). The well-formed characters and the freshness of ink bear proof to the mature skill of the printers. The frontispiece, depicting Buddha giving a message to his disciple Subhuti in the Jetavana while surrounded by listening Bodhisattvas, was superbly executed. The scroll is composed of six sheets, each one Chinese foot wide by two feet long. The characters on it are all printed by woodblocks of the same size, and the frontispiece is composed of a woodcut. The sheets were pasted together lengthwise to form a scroll. It is the oldest known block-printed book in the world, and the frontispiece probably the oldest known woodcut. The discovery of the *Diamond Sutra* proves beyond doubt that the art of block-printing was highly advanced in China in the middle of the 9th century. Its invention, therefore, must have been at a much earlier date.

The fact that the art of printing was invented in China before the 9th century is also indirectly proved by the block-printed scroll of *Dharani,* a Buddhist sutra containing more than 1,000 characters. This was done by order of the Japanese empress Shotoku. It is believed that as many as 1,000,000 copies of this scroll were printed and distributed, and that these copies were kept in small pagodas of monasteries, where some can be seen to this day. Said to have been printed in A. D. 770, about 100 years earlier than the *Diamond Sutra,* the *Dharani* was cut and printed rather crudely, indicating that the art of printing was still in its early stages. Scholars — Japanese scholars included — agree that the printing method for the *Dharani* came from China, and this is believable in view of the frequent cultural contacts between China and Japan in this period. This also proves that early in the 8th century printing had already been invented in China. Recently some researchers have put the printing of the *Dharani* at a much later date. But if this is true, it by no means upsets the claim that printing was current in China in the 8th century, since the claim is well supported by Tang records.

The most reliable of these Tang records, complete with the month and year of printing (Dec. 29, 835), is the memorial of Feng Su, military governor of Dongchuan Prefecture. He suggested in this memorial that private possession of calendar printing blocks should be forbidden, and he reported that in Jiannan, Liangchuan and Huannandao (now Sichuan, Jiangsu and Anhui provinces) calendars were printed every year by private blocks and sold all over the country before the official calendar was issued.

Almanac of the late Tang Dynasty

In a preface to *Chang Qing Ji* (*Anthology of Bai Juyi*), Yuan Zhen, a contemporary of Feng Su, said in January 825: "Books are copied and printed and sold in the market." From this, it is evident that not only calendars but also poems and essays were printed at the beginning of the 9th century.

In an article in his *Yi Ming Ji* (*One Man's Anthology*), Sikong Tu said he once collected money so that the monks of a certain monastery could print Buddhist scriptures. The article was written between 869 and 880, about the time it is thought that the printing of the *Diamond Sutra* took place. Sikong Tu also said that the monastery had previously kept printed Buddhist scriptures which were lost when Emperor Wu Zong banned Buddhism in 845. Obviously these Buddhist scriptures must have been printed prior to that date.

From these facts it is obvious that block printing was already quite popular in the early 9th century in China. Calendars, literary works and Buddhist scriptures were by then being printed. By the closing years of the Tang Dynasty, a wider range of printed matter was appearing. In his preface to *Jia Xun (Family Dictum)*, Liu Pin said that in 883, he saw many books in the bookshops of Cheng-du, most of them about divination, portents and dreams, miscellaneous subjects, and how to write Chinese characters. These, he said, were all block-printed books, but they were hardly legible. This statement points to the fact that printing by the end of the Tang Dynasty was practised in many areas of the country.

It is reasonable, therefore, to place the date for the invention of printing at the end of the 7th century or the beginning of the 8th century, during the reigns of emperors Gao Zong and Xuan Zong of the Tang Dynasty. Printing might even have developed earlier, but it is impossible to know the date for sure or to know the name of the inventor. For the invention of printing, like that of paper, was a result of the accumulated experience of many people, a gradual process evolved from rubbing and seal engraving.

From the writings of Feng Su and Liu Pin, the records of the Song Dynasty and the printed matter extant in the Tang Dynasty, we may infer that printing developed in and around Sichuan, which was subsequently a block-cutting during the Northern Song Dynasty (960-1127). Sichuan was a paper producing centre with a prosperous economy, and so it was in a favourable position for the invention of printing.

A considerable sum of money was needed to print a book, and nobody would be willing to have one printed unless there was a large demand. Calendars and books for learning how to write characters, both subjects of wide appeal, were the first to be printed. Books about divination, portents and dreams were also popular. The invention of printing, it seems, answered a need of the time.

Scholars in positions of power, however, were slow to shed their conservative attitude towards the new art. An instance of this occurred in 837 when Emperor Wen Zong of the Tang Dynasty erected stone classics to preserve knowledge instead of printing books to do so, even though printing was already in existence. But the followers of Buddhism saw printing a useful means for spreading their faith. They employed the art to print Buddhist writings in large numbers, which is why most of the oldest printed matter is Buddhist scriptures and Buddha's images. It was only from the late Tang Dynasty to the early period of the Five Dynasties that printing began to be used for books by scholars and men of letters. As for orthodox Confucian classics, these were not printed until the beginning of the 10th century, first at Kaifeng, sponsored by the prime minister, Feng Dao, and later in Chengdu, sponsored by Wu Zhaoyi.

The Development of Block Printing

From the very beginning of block printing, character cutting and picture engraving were closely associated. The *Diamond Sutra* of A. D. 868, with text and illustrations, is a good example of this. During the Tang Dynasty and the Five Dynasties, many single-sheet Buddhist pictures were printed with a text on the lower half of the sheet. Books such as the *San Li Tu* (*Three Classics Illustrated*), *Xuan He Bo Gu Tu* (*Xuanhe Reign Illustrated Record of Ancient Objects*), and *Zheng Lei Ben Cao* (*Reorganized Pharmacopoeia*) of the Song Dynasty had printed illustrations of various ancient things including clothes, utensils, plants and animals. There were also popular books and stories, such as the *New Illustrated Story About King Wu's Conquest of the Shangs* printed during the Zhizhi reign (1321-1323) of the Yuan Dynasty, that were like popular picture story books today, with a picture on the upper half of every page and the text on the lower half. *Da Guan Ben Cao* (*Daguan Reign Pharmacopoeia*) and *Zhao Cheng Zang* (*Zhaocheng Buddhist Scriptures*), printed during the Jin Dynasty (1115-1234), were also beautifully illustrated. The execution of the pictures showed superb craftsmanship.

But it was not until late in the Ming Dynasty, during the 17th century, that woodcutting attained artistic perfection. Novels and plays then had extremely fine illustrations, sometimes hundreds of them in a single book. A Ming Dynasty edition of *San Guo Yan Yi* (*Romance of the Three Kingdoms*), for example, has 240 pictures; and an edition of *Shui Hu Zhuan* (*Outlaws of the Marsh*) has more than 200. Bookstores in Nanjing, Suzhou and Jianyang printed many splendidly illustrated legends and miscellaneous ballads.

There were several well-known schools of engravers, including the Jian'an School, Jinling (Nanjing) School, and Xin'an School, and some individual engravers even achieved fame. Most of them were natives of Huizhou, Anhui Province — once a centre for woodcut artists. Just as literary works were illustrated, so were books on engineering and architecture, with charts and designs. *Mo Pu* (*Discourse on Ink*) by Fang Yulu, *Mo Yuan* (*Garden of Ink*) by Cheng Junfang, *Tian Gong Kai Wu* (*Expositions of the Works of Nature*) by Song Yingxing and *Nong Zheng Quan Shu* (*Complete Treatise on Agriculture*) by

Xu Guangqi, all printed during the Ming Dynasty, had beautiful pictures. *Chinese Woodcuts*, compiled by Lu Xun and Zheng Zhenduo, shows many examples of illustrations from these books.

Some people hold the incorrect idea that China learned book illustration from the West in relatively recent times. But the fact is that China had a tradition of lavish and superb book illustrations long before the 18th century. During the Qing Dynasty, some of the best-illustrated books included the *Gu Jin Tu Shu Ji Cheng* (*Collection of Books Ancient and Modern*), printed during Kang Xi's reign; and Xiao Yuncong's *Li Sao Quan Tu* (*Complete Illustrations for "The Lament"*) and a court edition of *Shou Shi Tong Kao* (*A Guide to Farming*), both printed during Qian Long's reign. It was not until the mid-19th century, when foreign aggression reduced China to a semi-feudal and semi-colonial state, that the art of picture engraving began to decline.

An important step in the development of block printing was marked by the invention of multi-colour printing during the 14th century. *The Annotations to the "Diamond Sutra"*, printed in 1340, is the earliest existing book printed with the method. The text was printed in red ink and the annotations in black; the frontispiece was also done in these two colours.

Multi-colour printing is a complex art, requiring great precision in workmanship for its execution. The greater the number of colours, the more essential the skill. The process of multi-colour printing began with two colours, red and black. By the early 17th century, five-colour printing was in use. Many printers during the Ming Dynasty were proficient in this art. Considerable progress in multi-colour printing was also made during the Qing Dynasty.

Multi-colour block printing was a combination of colour printing and woodcutting. The best early examples are *Shi Zhu Zhai Hua Pu* (*Ten-Bamboo Studio Painter's Manual*) and *Jian Pu* (*Ornamental Letter-Paper*), a collection of fancy note-papers. Each page is an object of art, showing a variety of colours and tones. Multi-colour block printing campares favourably with modern colour printing.

Chapter VI

The Invention of Movable-Type Printing and Its Development

The Invention of Movable-Type Printing

Like block printing, movable-type printing was invented by the Chinese, and in this, as in block printing, Europe was influenced by China.

Movable-type printing was invented in the 11th century by a Chinese worker named Bi Sheng. Of Bi Sheng's history we know little. His methods, however, was preserved and handed down to us through a book called *Meng Xi Bi Tan* (*Dream Stream Essays*) written by Shen Kuo (1031-1095), a Song scientist. The process is as follows:

Take sticky clay and cut into it characters as thin as the edge of a cash. Each character is formed as if it were a single type. Bake them in the fire to make them hard. Prepare an iron plate and cover it with a mixture of pine resin, wax and paper ashes. Make an iron frame the size of the text. Set the frame on the plate and place the type on it till the frame is full. Then put the plate near the fire to warm. When the wax is lightly melted, take a perfectly smooth board and rub it slightly over the surface so that the face of the type is level. The plate is then taken away

Bi Sheng (?-c. 1051)

to cool until the clay characters are fixed in place and are ready for printing. If two plates are in use alternately, with the one being put aside for type-setting while the other is being printed, the rate of printing will be faster. If any character that has not been made in advance is needed, it can be cut and baked immediately. When the printing is done, the plate is rewarmed and the clay type is taken away for the next printing.

Such was the earliest method for movable-type printing. Compared with movable-type printing today, it seems clumsy and primitive. But the underlying principles of casting, type-setting and printing were there, and the technique only remained to be improved.

Movable-type printing was not widely employed in China until long after it was invented; block printing still remained dominant. This was because the former took a lot more time to get ready and was convenient only when a large number of copies were to be printed.

"If one were to print only one or two copies," said Shen Kuo in appraising this method, "it would be neither simple nor convenient. But for printing hundreds or thousands of copies, it is amazingly quick."

Movable-type printing was not used extensively primarily because of the limited reading public. In feudal society reading was the privilege of a few. The demand for one particular book during any given period was almost always small, and book circulation was therefore slow. If thousands of copies of a book were printed, years might pass before they were all sold. It would be uneconomical, and no publisher would be willing to print so many. It would be equally uneconomical if too few books were printed with movable type so that the type would have to be reset for another printing when the stock ran out. In block printing this drawback did not exist. The blocks could be preserved and as many copies as needed could be produced whenever they were required. There was no stock-piling and no trouble of type-setting. Most of the publishers, therefore, preferred block printing.

The Development of Movable-Type Printing

Although movable-type printing was not as generally used as block printing, its use was continuous and it was continually improved.

It is said that many books were printed with movable type during the Song Dynasty, but none of them has been handed down to posterity. Some progress was made in the art of movable-type printing during the Yuan Dynasty. Tin was then used for the type, but this didn't work well because the tin did not hold ink readily and the type faces easily deteriorated during the course of use. But it is an indisputable fact that metal type was used in China in the 13th century.

Between 1312-13, during the Yuan Dynasty, Wang Zhen also created wooden type, which was a great improvement. His method for doing this was as follows: A wooden block was engraved with characters. The block was then cut with a small, fine-toothed saw until each character formed a separate piece. These separate pieces were then trimmed with a knife on each of their four sides until they were all exactly the same size and height. In setting, the type was placed in columns separated by bamboo strips. After the type had all been set in the form, the spaces were filled in with wooden plugs so that the type would be perfectly firm and would not move.

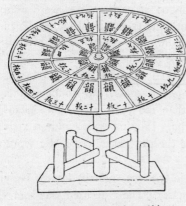

Revolving type-setting table invented by Wang Zhen

Wang Zhen also prescribed a standard number of characters for the movable type, with the most common characters being produced in the largest number. Furthermore, he created a type-setting device which made selection and composition easier. This type-setting device was a revolving table made of light wood, about seven Chinese feet in diameter. On the table was a round bamboo frame in which the type was kept. The table was divided into many compartments according to the arrangement in the *Book of Rhymes*. Individual characters were numbered and separated into the proper compartments. The most common characters were placed on another revolving table of the same size. Altogether more than 30,000 characters were placed on the two tables. Between them sat a man who turned the tables either to right or left to find and remove the desired type and place it in the "chase". Another man held the *Book of Rhymes* list and called for the desired type by number.

The type was placed from the "chase" onto a smooth, straight, dry block with the dimensions of a book page.

The block was edged on three of its four sides. An edge was attached to the fourth side after the frame was filled with type. For printings, the type had to be exactly even and level. Slivers of bamboo of various sizes were used for this purpose. Not until the type was absolutely even and firm was printing begun. Wang Zhen described his contribution to movable-type printing in his book, *A guide to Movable-type Printing*. His method was used in the printing of the *Jingde County Records*, with commendable results. This was more than 100 years before Europeans began to use movable type. Printing with hand-set type today is still basically like the method described by Wang Zhen.

Printing with movable type was practised extensively during the mid-Ming Dynasty. The type used was sometimes made of wood and sometimes of copper, which was a great improvement. The best-known printing houses of that time were the Huitongguan, Guipoguan and Lanxuetang in Wuxi (in Jiangsu Province), all of which used copper type. Unfortunately, their method was not recorded and there is no way of knowing how they improved the printing technique. The late period of the Ming Dynasty saw a good number of books that were printed with movable copper type. Even voluminous works, such as the *Taiping Imperial Encyclopedia*, were produced by this method. In the 17th century, movable wooden type was used in the printing of *Di Bao*, an official gazette of the Ming court.

Movable-type printing attained popularity between the 15th and 16th centuries, because social production had reached a high level of development at that time. And it is only natural that Wuxi should become a printing centre, it being located in the economically and culturally more developed southern part of the country.

During the Qing Dynasty, movable copper type continued to be used for printing books. In 1726, in the 4th year of Emperor Yong Zheng, the *Collection of Books Ancient and Modern* was printed. But, again, details of the printing method used are not known. The 39th year of Emperor Qian Long's reign (1774) saw the use of date wood for making the type used in printing the rare books taken from *the Yongle Encyclopedia*. These books were called the "collected gem editions". The procedure was under the direction of Jin Jian, who wrote about the method in great detail.

In place of the revolving tables, Jin Jian used wooden boxes. The type was kept in drawers in these boxes according to the arrangement in the *Book of Rhymes*. Jin Jian used this method to print over 100 different books known as the "Fine Editions from Wuyingdian". Wuyingdian was one of the halls in the Imperial Palace that was used as the general printing office for the Qing court. The editions of these books were many, but the best-known were the Suzhou edition and that of Hangzhou.

Movable wooden type was also extensively used outside of the court printing office during the Qing Dynasty. The 56th year of Emperor Qian Long's reign saw the first edition of *A Dream of Red Mansions* by Gao E and Cheng Weiyuan printed with wooden type. In the following year, a second edition was printed with some additions and deletions from the earlier edition. The two are respectively known as the "Cheng Edition A" and "Cheng Edition B". Movable clay type was also used with some success. During the reign of Emperor Dao Guang (1821-1850) Zhai Jingsheng, a native of Jingxian County, Anhui Province, succeeded in using more than 100,000 clay characters to print books such as the *Pedigree Records of the Zhais* and *Rudiments of the Clay Trial Edition,* a book about his printing method. These two books can still be found in some big libraries of China. By the middle decades of the 19th century, when the Occidental counterpart of the art of printing came to the Orient, Chinese printers adapted it for the printing of Chinese characters.

The Spread of Movable-
Type Printing

Chinese movable-type printing first reached Korea in the early 15th century. The Koreans used copper type, and technical improvements were made there by succeeding generations. Today, the old Korean books printed with movable copper type are still treasured objects. Wooden and iron movable types were sometimes also used in Korea.

The Japanese learned the art of movable-type printing from the Koreans. Their first book, *Gu Wen Xiao Jing* (*The Canon of Filial Piety in Ancient Script*), was printed in 1593 with wooden type faces, in imitation of the Korean copper type. By the mid-19th century the Japanese changed to the use of Occidental lead type, with marked improvement.

In Europe, movable type is said to have been invented in Germany by Johannes Gutenberg about 1450. But during the 12th and 13th centuries China and Europe had frequent contacts through the Middle East, and the Crusaders undoubtedly brought the method of block printing to Europe. Block printing in the Middle East, as everyone acknowledges, came from China.

During the Yuan Dynasty, after Europe had established direct contacts with China, many things Chinese found their way into Europe. It is highly probable that the Chinese technique, or at least principles, of movable-type printing came to Europe at this time. It seems that Gutenberg merely applied the Chinese principles to the German alphabet, and made some technical improvements. Europe was then in the critical stage of transition from feudalism to capitalism. In pursuit of knowledge, the nascent bourgeoisie raised a great demand for books. This stimulated the development of movable-type printing, for which the progress made in mechanical science during the 16th and 17th centuries prepared the ground.

Chapter VII

Books After the Invention of Printing

Works After the Invention of Printing

With the development of feudal society and the spread of knowledge, an increasing number of people became fired with the idea of becoming educated, and a great demand was raised for books. This stimulated the production of books by scholars and authorities in various fields. In the more than 900 years from the Song Dynasty to the late Qing Dynasty, books became so numerous that they would make "an ox that carried them sweat, or fill a house to the rafters". A glance at the book catalogues of different dynasties shows that the number of authors and their works increased with each generation.

During the Song Dynasty, scholars added *Mencius* to the dozen Confucian philosophical works (*The Book of Changes, The Book of History, The Book of Songs, Rites of the Zhou Dynasty, The Book of Rites, Records of Rites, Zuo Qiuming's Commentary on "The Spring and Autumn Annals", Gong Yang's Commentary on "The Spring Autumn Annals", Gu Liang's Commentary on "The Spring and Autumn Annals", Analects of Confucius, The Canon of Filial Piety* and *Literary Expositor*) designated by Tang scholars under the general title of "Twelve Classics". Under the comprehensive title of "Four Books" were grouped the *Great Learning, Doctrine of the Mean, Analects of Confucius* and *Mencius*. All these books were printed and reprinted during the Song Dynasty, and they became standard textbooks.

The Neo-Confucianism became the ruling ideology of the Southern Song Dynasty. Cheng Hao, Cheng Yi and Zhang Zai of the Northern Song, and Zhu Xi and Lu Jiuyuan of the Southern Song, were its originators. From the Yuan Dynasty onward the theories of the Zhu Xi School of Neo-Confucianism enjoyed the highest esteem of feudal rulers, and became the ruling ideology in the later stage of feudal society. In spite of all the controversies that developed around this Zhu Xi School, Neo-Confucianism held its ground and did not budge from its orthodox position. A galaxy of works were produced by scholars of Neo-Confucianism and those against it. The *Tong Zhi Tang Jing Jie* (*Collection of Monographs on the Classics of Tongzhi Hall*) is a bulky work, printed in series, that includes all the writings of the famous scholars of Neo-Confucianism. It was circulated in the name of Nalanchengde during the reign of Emperor Kang Xi of the Qing Dynasty. The *Huang Qing Jing Jie* (*Collection of Monographs on Classics*), compiled by Ruan Yuan during the reign of Jiaqing (1796-1820), consists of works in refutation of the Neo-Confucian School.

In the field of history, there were *Zi Zhi Tong Jian* (*History As a Mirror*), a famous chronological work by Sima Guang of the Song Dynasty, and *Tong Zhi* (*Historical Collections*), written by Zheng Qiao as a series of biographies, and *Wen Xian Tong Kao* (*A Comprehensive*

85

Study of Civilization), written in the wake of the *Tong Dian* (*Encyclopedia*) by Du You of the Tang Dynasty. The latter was a work by Ma Duanlin of the Yuan Dynasty, devoted to a study of cultural establishments, institutions and historical relics. In later years these three works were called the "three general histories".

As for archeology, a way was laid by Ouyang Xiu and Zhao Mingcheng of the Song Dynasty with their works, *Ji Gu Lu* (*Record of Ancient Stone Inscriptions*) and *Jin Shi Lu* (*Record of Inscriptions on Metal and Stone*). Meanwhile, there also appeared works devoted to the study of calligraphy and painting. In addition to these, local histories were compiled in many places during the Song Dynasty, and by the Ming-Qing period the number of such local histories increased enormously. These have provided us with the best material for research — into the history, economy, geography and culture of different localities in China.

In literature, during the Song Dynasty, there developed a special poetic form using sentence patterns based on song melodies from the Tang Dynasty, known as *ci*. During the Yuan Dynasty, plays developed out of the operas that played in singsong houses during the Song Dynasty. Bian Wen (literary performing pieces with words set to music) popular in the Tang period and ballads as heard in Tang temples and monasteries developed into a form of story-telling during the Song Dynasty. In addition to this, many stories told by the storytellers appeared in written form. And novels, based on these, were created during the Yuan Dynasty. And, during the Ming Dynasty, *Zhuan Qi* (novels written in a historical style) was developed out of the plays of the Yuan period. Apart from these, there were a good many personal collections or selections of writings by individual scholars that included their poems, *ci*, ballads, prose pieces, notes and letters. By the late Ming Dynasty, the number of personal collections and selections of writings that were printed by individuals were so numerous that almost every noted scholar had selected or collected works of his own produced. Though quite a few were done in the finest vein in terms of their academic value, many were worthless, full of stale and outworn views.

The science and technology books were few in comparison to those mentioned above, and very few have been preserved. But in the field of agriculture there were such famous works as *Nong Sang Ji Yao* (*Fundamentals of Agriculture and Sericulture*), written in the Yuan Dynasty, and *Nong Zheng Quan Shu* (*Complete Treatise on Agriculture*) by Xu Guangqi of the Ming Dynasty. In addition, there were works on Chinese architecture during the Song Dynasty, such as *Ying Zao Fa Shi* (*Building Formulas*) by Li Jie; *Tian Gong Kai Wu* (*Expositions of the Works of Nature*), a monumental work on technology by Song Ying-xing of the Ming Dynasty; and the world-famous pharma-copoeia *Ben Cao Gang Mu* (*Compendium of Materia Medica*) by Li Shizhen of the Ming Dynasty. Towards the end of the Ming Dynasty, the spread of Catholicism in China brought with it scientific works from the West. These were soon rendered into Chinese. Meanwhile, works of mathe-matics, mechanics and physics from Europe also began to enter China.

Along with this, the practice of compiling voluminous works began in the Song Dynasty. Among the oldest of these was the *Ru Xue Jing Wu* (*Confucianist Anecdotes*) as it is known to this day. The mid-Ming period saw a grad-ual increase in the number of such books, and the pace accelerated beginning in the reign of Qian Long of the Qing Dynasty. There were many voluminous works that were characterized by their pithy content, such as *Shi Li Ju Cong Shu* (*Books of the Shiliju Study*), *Zhi Bu Zu Zhai Cong Shu* (*Books of the Zhibuzu Study*), *Yue Ya Tang Cong Shu* (*Books of the Yueya Hall*), and *Jing Xun Tang Cong Shu* (*Books of the Jingxun Hall*). The *Yan Yi Zhi Lin* (*Journal and Miscellany of Yanyi*), *Yong Jia Cong Shu* (*Books of the Yongjia Hall*) and the like were works compiled of writings from specific localities. The *Shi San Jing Zhu Shu* (*Thirteen Classics with Collected Commentaries*), *Er Shi Si Shi* (*Twenty-Four Dynastic Histories*) and *Yan Shi Wen Fang Xiao Shuo* (*Anecdotes from the Yan Study*) were works respectively devoted to specific fields of academic studies. A summary of these is seen in the work *Cong Shu Zong Lu* (*A Critical Catalogue of Books*) compiled by Shanghai Library.

The period from the Song Dynasty on saw not only an increasing number of personal works by scholars but also an increasing number of books compiled under the orders of imperial rulers. These were stamped with "imperial printing", "imperial edition", "compiled under orders of the court", "with His Majesty's sanction" and the like, even though they were actually products of the collective effort of a good many scholars. Four of them, known as the "four great ancient works" of the Song Dynasty, were the *Tai Ping Yu Lan* (*Taiping Imperial Encyclopedia*), *Wen Yuan Ying Hua* (*Choice Blossoms from the Garden of Literature*) and *Tai Ping Guang Ji* (*Taiping Miscellany*), compiled under the order of Emperor Tai Zong, and the *Ce Fu Yuan Gui* (*Encyclopedia of History*), compiled under the order of Emperor Zhen Zong.

The *Taiping Imperial Encyclopedia* is a bulky work

of 1,000 *juan*. Composed of 55 parts with a specific number of sections in each part, the work introduces an abundance of material taken from more than 1,000 old history books and classics. It includes many *lu shi* (poems of eight lines with strictly regulated tones and syllables), *fu* (descriptive prose interspersed with verse), *ming* (inscribed writings), *zhen* (compositions of admonition and exhortation) and other miscellaneous writings. Because most of the original works used in its compilation have been lost, it has proved to be of great benefit to researchers, even though the pieces used are often incomplete. Such books as *Fan Zi Ji Ran* (*The Book of Master Ji Ni*) and *Fan Sheng Zhi Shu* (*The Book of Fan Shengzhi*), known for their treatment of farming techniques, as well as a number of old history books that have been lost are known today only because of their preservation in the great *Taiping Imperial Encyclopedia*.

Since the Song Dynasty, the *Taiping Imperial Encyclopedia* had had more than a dozen editions. For the convenience of book lovers and researchers, a reduced format of this voluminous work was produced by Zhonghua Shuju (China Publishing House) in 1959, with each page comprising two columns and every two pages combined into one.

Choice Blossoms from the Garden of Literature is a collection of more than 20,000 pieces of writing from the works of more than 2,000 writers beginning in the Liang period (502-557) and extending through the Five Dynasties. Totalling 1,000 *juan* it is classified into 38 sections including *fu* and odes. The largest part is by writers of the Tang Dynasty. But much of the work is composed of public announcements, letters, government proclamations and despatches used in seeking official careers. Despite this, the work is useful because it has preserved many documents of historical interest that would have otherwise been lost. In 1966, a photolithographic edition of this work was published by the China Publishing House.

The *Encyclopedia of History* consists of more than 1,000 parts summarizing the "17 histories". It gives a wide coverage to the lives of historical personages, ministers and monarchs, and relates events from remote antiquity through the Five Dynasties. The work provides an abundance of material for textual research into the rare books that existed before the Northern Song Dynasty. Only a few old copies of this book in its original form still exist. In 1959, on the basis of a Ming Dynasty edition that had been textually corrected, a new photolithographic edition was issued by the China Publishing House.

The Taiping Miscellany consists of 500 *juan*, and is a large collection of old stories and anecdotes from the various dynasties. Many ancient writings and documents taken from scattered pieces of scroll writing are preserved in this work. It thus provides valuable material for research into China's ancient literature.

The *Yongle Encyclopedia,* compiled under the orders of Ming Dynasty Emperor Cheng Zu, was one of the largest encyclopedias ever produced. During the first year of Yongle reign, Emperor Cheng Zu ordered the Hanlin academician, Xie Jin, and others to compile a classified work. It was completed the following year and named *Wen Xian Da Cheng (Compendium of Documents).* But the emperor thought it was too condensed. He therefore gathered more than 3,000 editors and writers to design another work. With material collected from 7,000-8,000 books, the group completed their encyclopedia in the sixth year of Yongle's reign (1408). The work comprised 22,877 *juan*, in addition to 60 *juan* of contents, bound into 11,095 volumes. It was called the *Yongle Encyclopedia*. Its contents were arranged according to phonetic rhymes, covering astronomy, geography, biographies, memorable events and famous sites, stories and strange tales, heresies, poems and ballads, etc. They were separately copied in seal-style calligraphy, official script, regular script and cursive script. The parts of the work that still exist are extremely valuable because they contain a wealth of material from books that have been lost. But the work was too gigantic an undertaking to warrant block printing, and so the single copy was kept in Wenyuange Library in Nanjing. Later, during the Jiaqing reign, another copy of the work was made. The original copy was moved to the capital for safe keeping after the completion of the Imperial Palace in Beijing, but it was reportedly destroyed in fire some time afterwards. The reproduced copy was kept in the Hanlin Academy during the Qing Dynasty.

In 1900, when the combined forces of eight imperialist powers occupied Beijing, vandals burned and plundered the invaluable work. Only 64 volumes were saved by the Chinese. These were moved into the Metropolitan Library (now Beijing Library). After the founding of the People's Republic of China in 1949, the government engaged in laborious inquiries to trace the existing segments that had been taken to other countries. By 1959, it had been able to buy back 215 volumes. In September 1960, after 20 months of preparation and planning by the China Publishing House, a photolithographic edition of the work was completed, including the regained copies and photographic copies of sections retained in other countries. But this was only one-thirtieth of the original encyclopedia as it existed before the eight powers' vandalization.

During the reigns of Qing emperors Kang Xi and Qian Long, many books were compiled and printed. Most of those compiled in Kang Xi's time are important references for the study of the country's ancient literature. Included are the *Kang Xi Dictionary, Pei Wen Yun Fu* (*Repertory of Classics*), *Yuan Jian Lei Han* (*The Deep Mirror of Classified Knowledge*), *Quan Tang Shi* (*The Tang Poetry*) and *Li Dai Shi Yu* (*Notes on Poetry Through the Ages*).

The *Collection of Books Ancient and Modern,* compiled also during the reign of Emperor Kang Xi, is a famous encyclopedia that was copiously illustrated. It classifies the different branches of knowledge into departments, and includes abundant examples, commentaries and notes. The classification is on the basis of history, institutions, economy, geography, astronomy, fauna and flora, various kinds of instruments and household utensils, and writings introducing foreign countries. Completed in the fourth year of the Yongzheng reign (1726), the work was printed in movable copper type. By the end of the Qing Dynasty there were two editions, one put out by letterpress and the other by photolithography. Before the outbreak of the War of Resistance Against Japan, a miniature edition of the work was brought out by the China Publishing House.

The Complete Library of the Four Treasures of Knowledge is a voluminous work compiled during the reign of Emperor Qian Long. It included 3,457 books, and consisted of 79,070 *juan* that were divided into four categories — classics, history, philosophical works and literary works. Beginning in 1773, the work took 10 years to complete. The 10 years also saw the completion of the 200-

juan Critical Catalogue of "*The Complete Library of the Four Treasures of Knowledge*". Seven sets of *The Complete Library of the Four Treasures of Knowledge*, each comprising 36,000 volumes, were copied by hand. Of these only four remain.

The *Four Treasures* is a great encyclopedia of China's feudal culture. It includes material from many famous ancient books, several hundred of which have been lost, as well as material from such famous works as the *Yongle Encyclopedia*. During the Qing Dynasty, however, few people ever came into contact with the work, since it was kept in the Imperial Palace and government institutions under strict restrictions on readership. All readers, almost without exception, knew of it by its contents as listed in the *Critical Catalogue of "The Complete Library of the Four Treasures of Knowledge"*. This had a comparatively detailed introduction and appraisal of all the books included in the *Four Treasure*. As a result, the influence of the *Catalogue* far exceeded that of the *Four Treasures*, and people in subsequent generations have considered the *Catalogue* the greater landmark work for academic studies.

From the early days of feudalism, books were collected and compiled by rulers with an eye towards further strengthening their own rule. They thus seized every opportunity to eliminate the works of those where views were alien to their own. In this, the Qing emperors Kang Xi, Yong Zheng and Qian Long were no exception. They committed several dozen literary inquisitions. Digging into the available writings and acting on clandestine information, they collected all works containing "possible slanderous" words and sentiments against national oppression and political tyranny. They rounded up the authors, killing some, jailing others, and sending some into exile. The victims even included some descendants and kinsmen of the writers.

Under the manipulation of emperors Kang Xi, Yong Zheng and Qian Long attacks were launched against such noted authors as Zhuang Tinglong, Lu Liuliang and Xu Shukui. Books by them were either burned or suppressed. The specific regulations that provided for the compilation of the *Four Treasures* included a long list of as many as 3,000 books that the emperor wanted banned. Not only were these books destroyed, but the printing blocks for their duplication were burned by the central authorities. Documents show that in the period from December of the 38th year of Qian Long's reign to October of the 45th year there were altogether 52,480 printing blocks for "undesirable" works that were collected and burned during the compilation of the *Four Treasures*. Then, in the 11 months from November in the 45th year to September in the 46th, there were additional 15,759 printing blocks that were confiscated. As a result, many outstanding works by ancient writers have been lost.

Though the figures cited above are fragmentary and incomplete, they still provide us with an amazing picture of how extensive was the vandalization. What is more, outrageous revisions and deletions were made in the writings chosen for the *Four Treasures,* leaving them widely different from their original form. This was particularly true of the works of the Song and Ming dynasties. The *Four Treasures* thus shows the repressive hand of the ruling class in its attempts to enforce ideological control over the people's knowledge.

Elementary Knowledge of the Editions of Early Books

With the invention of printing, the way was opened for the publication of a multitude of works under the same title and in different editions. Printed books of the same title are largely differentiated in the value of their contents by perfect texts in contrast with imperfect ones, and in the standard of their printing by the techniques used and quality of proofreading. Thus, when it comes to reading a book of a certain edition or printing, conscientious readers often make a choice as to its merit. Knowledge in regard to this is an established science known as textual research.

According to their appearance in different dynasties, old books of China are largely divided into those of Song printings, Yuan printings, Ming printings and Qing printings. And, taking into account the different reign years under various dynasties, they are subdivided into books of the Northern Song Dynasty printing and the Southern Song Dynasty printing; the Chunhua printing of the Northern Song; the Chunxi printing of the Southern Song; the Zhizheng printing and Dade printing of the Yuan; the Yongle printing, Hongzhi printing and Jiajing printing of the Ming; and the Kang Xi printing and Qian Long printing of the Qing.

The old books are also sometimes judged by the social status of the initiator of their printing in each historical period, to determine whether they were produced as official printings, home printings and bookshop printings. Official printing refers to books printed by relevant authorities at various levels, including those printed in the name of the throne, known as books of the imperial household.

Before the Ming Dynasty the only official printing books were those produced by relevant authorities, both at the central and local levels. But during the Ming Dynasty there were a number of books printed by the imperial household, although more were officially authorized print-ings. By the Qing Dynasty, books printed by the imperial household numbered more than those printed by official authorization.

The books of home printing were those produced by scholars or men of letters. Because of their special inter-ests, they had books printed in specific academic fields where they had attained expertise. Books such as those as of the Huang Shanfu printing during the Song Dynasty and the You Jujing printing during the Ming Dynasty were known by the names of the individuals who produced them. Home printing originated in the collected writings of He Ning and the *Chan Yue Ji* (*Chanyue Anthol-ogy*) of Monk Guan Xiu, written during the Five Dynas-ties. After the Song Dynasty, a growing number of peo-ple issued home printing books. But in most cases, only one or two titles were published by an individual, although there were a few home publishers who produced several hundred. The bookshop type of printing was produced by book sellers or bookstores. They were known by the sellers' names or those of the bookstores.

Among these three categories of printed matter, offi-cial books, especially those by the imperial household and the central government, usually were of a comparatively higher technical standard. But books of home printing sometimes were on a higher plane than the official ones in terms of content and academic importance. Shoddy work was often seen in the products of bookshop printing. Here the printers, with their eyes on quick sales, allowed poor workmanship and inferior material to be used. Yet the book sellers of the time, by their printing of books on general topics, such as textbooks, readers, reference books, novels, plays and storytellers' books, did more than anyone else to spread knowledge and folk literature among the Chinese people.

Old books are also sometimes classified by place of printing. And they can be classified according to inks — vermillion, blue and graphite; according to the number of lines on a page; according to those books carrying notes, commentaries and further commentaries. In short, many and varied are the ways to classify books of different printings.

As we have seen, there were also the many different types of printing — block printing and the movable wooden copper, clay and lead type faces. But among the country's old books made from engraved blocks, those of Song Dynasty printing are the most treasured.

They were the nearest in form to the original hand-written scrolls, since their texts were, in most cases, taken from hand-written copies which had undergone a strict process of checking. Today, when we hardly have any more old hand-written manuscripts, these Song Dynasty books have become invaluable materials for the study of ancient and mediaeval culture. Also, the Song Dynasty books were engraved and printed with such fine workmanship that they are looked upon as objects of art. And, of course, after 800 to 900 years of preservation they are the rarest treasures.

The blocks used in printing were generally rectangular in shape, with a maximum size of 18 by 8 inches. The sheet of impression paper was printed on one side only. The space enclosed by the marginal lines is called the "block face" — the single lines being single-line margins and the double lines, double-line margins. The space outside the margins is known as the "heavenly head" above, and the "earthly foot" below, respectively. The lines ruling the text into columns are called the "borders". The narrow column in the middle of the "block face", at which the sheet is folded to form two pages, is called the "heart of the block". This is where the title or simplified title of the book, the volume and page numbers are put, or sometimes the number of characters on the leaf and the engraver's name. About one quarter of the distance from the upper margin, at the "heart of the block", is a symbol called a "fish tail"; sometimes there is another one at a corresponding distance from the bottom margin. Instead of a "fish tail", a horizontal line may be drawn. Sometimes a line is drawn at the "heart of the block" joining the two "fish tails" and extending to the upper and lower margins. If the line is thin, it is called a "small black mouth"; if it is thick, it is called a "big black mouth"; if there is no line, it is called a "white mouth". The basic form of a printed sheet and these technical terms are largely retained in modern books printed by letterpress.

The outstanding feature of Northern Song printing is the bold characters in free strokes, neatly spaced. The "heart of the block" which has a "white mouth" is inscribed with the number of characters on the sheet, the title and number of the chapter, and the engraver's name. During the Southern Song Dynasty, a new form gradually evolved. The characters looked much more elegant and were more closely spaced. Books printed in smaller characters appeared in greater numbers. The "white mouth" was replaced by a "big black mouth". The number of characters or the cutter's name were cut in such a way that, when printed, the words would appear in white on a black background. The "black mouth" method was practised by printers in the Yuan and Ming dynasties, up until the time of Ming emperor Jia Qing (early 16th century) when the style of characters of the Northern Song Dynasty and the "white mouth" were reverted to. The significance of Song printing lies in the fact that it laid the technical foundations for the development of a variety of new forms of printing.

The Bound-Volume Form

The appearance of the bound-volume form, which superseded scrolls, is closely related to block printing. We can even say that block printing was the principal condition for the appearance of the bound-volume form of books throughout the world.

But such books did not take their present form overnight. The earliest printed book, the *Diamond Sutra* (A.D. 868), was printed on a scroll. It took more than 100 years for the book to evolve from the scroll form to the bound-volume form.

At the initial stage of block-printing, the sheets were pasted together to make a long scroll. Later, because this was inconvenient to handle, the scroll gave place to "leaf binding" and "whirlwind binding". But it was too easy for whirlwind-bound books to become broken at the pleats, or folds. By the 10th century, someone had thought of a way to paste the edges of the pleats so that the leaves would not scatter if a break occurred. And since the sheet was printed on one side only, the exposure of an unprinted side indicated when a pleat had broken. This new method of pasting the pleats was the "butterfly binding".

The sheets were folded in the middle, with the two printed pages of the same sheet "face to face", and the unprinted pages "back to back". The centre lines where the sheets were folded were then pasted onto a wrapping cover. When the book was opened for reading, the entire sheet of text was revealed, with its centre stuck at the back like a butterfly with wings spread. Thus, the first bound-volume form appeared.

Butterfly binding

For books with a butterfly binding, thick paperboards were used for the front and back covers. Sometimes they were bound with cloth or brocade, and looked somewhat like modern cloth bindings. Where the sheets were pasted was called the "back of the book". The unpasted side was called the "mouth of the book". The upper part was called the "head of the book"; and the lower part, the "root of the book". Books were placed on a shelf with their mouths down and their backs up.

"Butterfly binding" originated during the Five Dynasties and was generally used during the Song Dynasty. But beginning in the Yuan Dynasty, this form of binding was gradually replaced by wrapped-back bindings. One defect of butterfly binding was that after every two pages of printed material there were two blank pages that had to be turned over in order to reach the next printed two. Improvement was obviously necessary. If the folded sheets were pasted at the page margin instead of at the folds, then only the sides with printing on them would appear and the reader could peruse the book uninterruptedly. A

Wrapped-back binding

new method, the "wrapped-back binding" as it came to be known, did away with the obvious shortcomings of the butterfly binding and soon completely replaced it.

At first, books with wrapped-back binding were shelved in the same way as books with butterfly binding. But the "mouth of the book" which was now the heart of the text, constantly rubbed against the shelf, and was quickly damaged. To avoid this, books were placed flat on the shelf. The covers therefore no longer warranted hard material and soft covers came into use.

Both methods of binding entailed a lot of pasting which took much time. The next improvement over the wrapped-back-binding method made use of the more than ample margins of each page. Small holes were pierced along this space and a paper "string" was put through the holes and tied so that the sheets would not become loose. The book was then wrapped in covers so that it looked exactly like one bound with the wrapped-back-binding method. This method remained the common one throughout the Yuan and Ming dynasties.

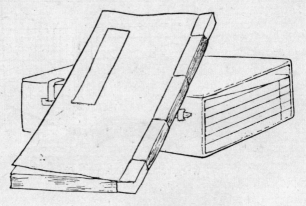

Thread-stitching

Thread stitching also seems to have been in use at a very early date. Some of the ancient hand-written books discovered in Dunhuang are said to have been stitched by thread. But this ancient method is not known to us in any detail.

The modern method of thread stitching was first employed in the 15th and 16th centuries, during the Ming Dynasty. The wrapping of a single sheet of paper over the back was dispensed with. The sheets were so arranged that the mouth of the book and the lower margins alined in their respective positions. A cover was placed on top of the pages and another on the bottom. All edges except the one forming the mouth (i.e. the heart of the text) were trimmed. Pinholes, generally four, sometimes six or eight in number depending on the size of the book, were put along the margin so as to let the thread through. Then the pages with the two covers were tied together with the thread. Books of exceptional value were bound at the corners with brocade to prevent them from being damaged by rubbing. When an old book was rebound, fresh paper was inserted between every two pages of each leaf before it was tied together.

Since the covers of these books were soft, they could not stand erect but were laid flat on a shelf, sometimes as many as several dozens of volumes forming a pile. To take them out and to put them back was a lot of trouble. In libraries where books were frequently used, the difficulty was most keenly felt. Accordingly, these thread-stitched books were eventually encased in cardboard boxes and sometimes they were cloth-bound so that they could stand erect on a shelf. The boxes were known as book clothes.

After the bound volume appeared, the content of books began to take a definite order, largely evolved from the content of old books; and this order is generally followed in books of today, though the terms are somewhat different. On the outside of a modern book is a sheet of paper thicker than the paper used for the main part of the book. This is called the cover. Its old equivalent was book clothes. Under the front cover is a blank sheet — the fly leaf in a modern book. The modern title page was once called the inner cover. After this, the preface, contents, main text, appendix, postscript and back cover, are practically the same in modern books as they were in the old books.

Chapter VIII

Contemporary Books and Modern Printing

The Adoption of Mechanized Printing

Highly-developed Western printing techniques have been introduced into China in modern times. Though there are great technological differences between Western printing and the handicraft printing process that originated in China, the general principles are the same.

The invention of movable lead type in the West, as has already been said, took place under the influence of Chinese printing techniques. When Gutenberg began to use movable type of the West, he advanced the technique by developing a unique primitive printing press. In time, technological improvements turned this into a giant mechanized one that did the major part of the work mechanically, including letter cutting and casting, type-setting, printing and binding. Embodying the development of highly specialized technology, modern printing makes use of all the achievements and knowledge of physics, mechanics and chemistry.

To avoid damaged letters, ready types are rarely used today in movable type printing. In printing books and newspapers, all modern printing houses make plates from the movable type that is cast anew for each operation, and the printing is done from the plates rather than the type itself. Strictly speaking, modern printing is therefore a merger of movable type with the plates made from it, rather than a simple, direct use of the former.

In modern printing, the whole process involves type casting, composing, checking, moulding matrices, making lead plates, make-up, printing and binding. In the case of printing pictures, the process involves, in the main, engraving and making process plates. Chromatographic printing uses coloured plates that are made separately for every single colour.

Modern lead type came into use in China about 130 years ago. In the early 19th century, European missionaries in China began to print Chinese books on Western printing presses and with lead type. In 1819 the first Chinese Bible was printed by letterpress in Malacca. After the Opium War of 1840, printing shops using movable lead type in Chinese characters were set up in Macao, Hongkong, Ningbo, Shanghai and other places. These were operated by foreign missionaries to publish religious pamphlets and books and to promote the material civilization of the West. This was the time when imperialism actively penetrated China and when the Chinese people began to resist imperialist aggression. Under such circumstances, the broad masses of people paid little heed to and saw no significance in the Western techniques.

But following the Second Opium War of 1856-60, launched by British and French imperialism, the Chinese people increasingly began to raise demands for political reform. Many intellectuals with bourgeois democratic ideas came to see the great significance of publications in influencing people's thinking. They set about publishing newspapers, magazines and books to provide information on bourgeois democracy and the need for political reforms. From 1860 onwards, modern printing shops and houses using the Western methods were established, and lead type gradually came into use in China. This was followed by the introduction of zinc plates, boxwood plates, and copper process plates, as well as a gradual adoption of new equipment such as mechanical hand printing presses, gas-powered rotary presses and type-casting machines.

During this same period, lithographic printing was adopted and used alongside lead type. Following the first use in China of lithographic printing (for religious pictures only) by the Shanghai Tusanwan Press in 1874, the first lithographic press — the Dianshizhai Lithographic Press — was opened in Shanghai by British businessmen in 1879. The British publishing company catered to the interests of a number of intellectuals, especially candidates in civil examinations, and reprinted ancient books such as the *Kang Xi Dictionary* by lithographic process method. These books amassed them a large fortune. Subsequently, money was invested in lithographic printing by Chinese capitalists. They set up presses, such as the Tongwen Shuju, Baishi Shanfang, Zhongxi Wucai Shuju, and Wenming Shuju. Wenming Shuju was equipped with up-to-date lithographic machines, and did fine work in printing pictorials and maps. By the beginning of the 20th century, the letterpress and lithographic techniques for printing books had become so popular that traditional Chinese block printing and movable type were relegated to a secondary position.

At the beginning of the present century, large publishing houses, such as the Commercial Press, Wenming Shuju and Zhonghua Shuju, had their own printing presses. Newspapers, like *Shen Bao* (*Shanghai Gazette*), *Xinwen*

Bao (*News Gazette*) and *Shi Bao* (*Times*), also engaged in the printing business. These establishments published many books and magazines, including academic studies. The printing techniques also steadily improved. In addition to the letterpress and lithography, there were intaglio and collotype presses. Skilled workmanship was evident in the single-colour pictures and fine coloured art reproductions that were produced. To this day, these reproductions of calligraphy and paintings by ancient and contemporary artists are treasured works of art.

After the establishment of the People's Republic of China in 1949, printing industry greatly expanded. The People's Government saw to it that necessary adjustments and reforms were made in the printing industry. Many provinces and cities established printing houses of their own. Furthermore, a number of printing houses began to operate with matrices and lead types in the languages of China's ethnic minorities. Offset printing and photogravure printing became popular, and improvements were made in the technique of photolithography and etched plates. This enabled Chinese printers to produce fine pictorials and pictures from their presses.

In order to train the needed personnel for the country's printing industry, professional schools and research institutions were established. Recent years have also seen the gradual adoption of phototype setting. Overall computerization of printing is even being considered. But the use of computers involves the solving of problems related to the Chinese language, with its complicated forms of characters and large numbers of homonyms. To that end, initial results have been achieved in research work. Moreover, as photo processing and plate making are now undertaken with the aid of colour scanners, quality printing is assured.

Success has also been achieved in making photopolymer plates. Made of low-cost materials, simple in operation and highly efficient when used, photopolymer plates do not cause lead poisoning and are good for ink printing. No sophisticated equipment is required when they are used to replace lead, zinc and copper plates. Great vistas have been opened by photo typesetting machines, and automatic binding is taking the place of hand work in binding books.

Books and Publication in Modern Times

Books and book publication experienced radical changes after the introduction of Western printing techniques. Now books appeared introducing new ideas on democracy, modern science and technology. Moreover, books were produced in much greater numbers.

China's feudal economy had begun to experience a process of disintegration following the invasion of imperialist forces after the Opium War. With its door closed to the outside world, the feudal empire was gradually becoming reduced to the status of a semi-feudal and semi-colonial country. The situation provided great impetus for the Chinese people to carry out an incessant struggle against imperialism and its Chinese lackeys.

With the growth of revolutionary struggles, there were profound changes taking place in book publication, both in form and content. The new books marked a world of difference from the books published in the past.

First, many foreign books were published that introduced the history of foreign countries, and books on geography, natural science and technology from other countries were translated into Chinese. The Beijing Tong Wen Guan (founded in 1862) and the Translation Bureau (formed in 1867) of the Kiangnan Arsenal and Dockyard in Shanghai were the first companies established to supply such translations. Run by the government, they produced a large number of books in translation. These initiated people into the mysteries of science and technology from the West. Meanwhile there were also some foreign missionaries who provided translations in order to propagate Western civilization and their religious beliefs throughout the country.

Foreign books were also translated into Chinese by individual translators from 1884 onwards, following the end of the Sino-French War. Books giving information on the politics of bourgeois democracy, bourgeois economics, and the ideas and philosophy of the bourgeois revolution appeared. The most influential among these individual translators was a man named Yan Fu. He translated *Evolution and Ethics* by Thomas Henry Huxley, *The Spirit of Laws* by Charles Louis de Secondat Montesquieu, Adam Smith's *The Wealth of Nations* and Herbert Spencer's *The Principles of Sociology*. The new ideas presented in these books shocked the ideological world in China at that time. Of almost as much significance was Ma Junwu's translation of *Social Contract* by Jean Jacques Rousseau. This work provided powerful revolutionary impetus to the idea of establishing a bourgeois republic in place of the monarchic system of the time.

By the beginning of the 20th century, translations of Western literature had become current. The first work of Western literature to gain people's attention was a translation of *The Lady of the Camellias* by Alexandre Dumas,

110

done by Lin Shu in 1894. Following this was his 1901 translation of Harriet Beecher Stowe's *Uncle Tom's Cabin,* a work that evoked the deepest sympathy among the oppressed Chinese by its exposition of American atrocities of racial discrimination. A significant work in the history of Chinese publication, it also gave great impetus to the development of patriotism in China.

The development of printing and the political struggles of the time also led to the appearance of newspapers and magazines. The first of these were used by European missionaries for religious propaganda. They included *Cha Shi Su Mei Yue Tong Ji Zhuan (An Investigation of Life),* a monthly and the earliest Chinese magazine. It was launched in 1815 by foreign businessmen in Malacca. Another was *Dong Xi Yang Kao Mei Yue Tong Ji Zhuan (A Study of the East and West).* This, too, was a monthly periodical. It started publication in 1833 in Guangzhou. There was space for news reports in both of these monthlies. In addition, many newspapers and magazines were inaugurated in Hongkong, Ningbo and Shanghai after the Opium War. These included *Zhongwai Xinbao (News of China and the West),* published in Honkong and the first daily printed in Chinese; and *Shen Bao (Shanghai Gazette), founded in* 1872, a paper of weighty importance at the time.

Apart from foreign missionaries and businessmen running newspapers, periodicals and magazines, there were also newspapers founded by Chinese. These included *Zhaowen Daily,* founded in 1873 in Hankou, and *Zhongwai Jiwen (World Bulletin),* a magazine launched in 1895 by the Learn-To-Be-Strong Society of Beijing. After the Sino-Japanese War of 1894, Chinese newspapers and magazines run by Chinese became the rule. This was a time when the Reform Movement of 1898 was at a high tide. Newspapers and magazines launched to promote reform were established in various places throughout the country. Among these were *Shiwu Bao* (*Contemporary Affairs*) and *Qiang Xue Bao* (*Learn-To-Be-Strong Journal*), both of which exerted a strong influence on the Reform Movement.

After the failure of the Reform Movement, a bourgeois democratic revolutionary movement took its place. This movement propagated its ideas on democratic revolution through newspapers and magazines such as the *Zhongguo Ribao* (*China Daily*), *Su Bao* (*Jiangsu News*), *Min Bao* (*People's Journal*), *Xing Shi* (*Awakened Lion*), *Zhejiang Chao* (*Zhejiang Tide*) and *Guocui Xuebao* (*Gem of National Culture*). In opposition to these journals of the revolutionists, newspapers like *Xinmin Congbao* (*New People's Journal*) and *Qing Yi Bao* (*Honest Opinion*) were published by the reformists. The proliferation of newspapers, magazines and periodicals during this time was unprecedented. The situation was not experienced again until the advent of the anti-imperialist, anti-feudal May 4th Movement in 1919.

Along with these news and political organs, there were also many scientific and technical journals and papers giving information on industry and commerce. In addition, newspapers, literary gazettes, journals, magazines and pictorials were published with the aim of educating the common masses, including women and children.

Book publication in China, then operating in the same way as other manufacturing and industrial enterprises, was under capitalist management. Beside the letter cutting shops of old there arose new publication centres, reinforced by new technologies in printing. Some publishing houses engaged in the publishing of new books and some bookstores dealt in books printed by letterpress or lithographic processes.

But, as characterized by semi-feudal and semi-colonial cultures, most of the books that were published consisted of those related to bourgeois culture or of book reproductions from the old, feudal Chinese society. To some extent, even these, however, played a role in advancing and popularizing culture.

With the conclusion of the May 4th Movement, in 1919, interest quickly developed in studying and propagating Marxism-Leninism. Within six months, China had more than 200 newspapers and periodicals that openly advocated or were friendly to socialism. A guiding role in the socialist revolutionary movement was played by periodicals such as *Xin Qing Nian* (*New Youth*), *Meizhou Pinglun* (*Weekly Review*), *Xiangdao* (*Guide*), *Xiangjiang Pinglun* (*Xiangjiang Review*), and *Zhongguo Qingnian* (*Chinese Youth*), all of them either initiated by or under the influence of the Chinese Communist Party. Many books advocating Marxism-Leninism and making studies of the developing Chinese revolution were brought out by printers in Shanghai and other parts of the country.

Following the failure of the great revolution of 1927, Chiang Kai-shek usurped state power and ruthlessly suppressed the revolutionary forces. He saw to it that revolutionary books were banned, and either confiscated or burned. But the revolutionary fire could not be put out. Under the leadership of the Communist Party, the people were politically awakened. They established revolutionary bases, followed by the founding of the Soviet Republic of China in the mountain regions of Hunan, Jiangxi and Fujian provinces. In these places a network of primary and middle schools to educate the labouring people were set up. Under the Soviet power, political writings and textbooks for school education, such as *An Elementary Introduction to Marxism, Lectures on Class Struggle, Education Under the Soviet Power, Readers for Children, Young People's Textbooks, Readers for Workers and Peasants*, etc., were issued.

Newspapers and periodicals were issued in different places, including the border regions, by both the central and local authorities. One of these was the fairly important *Hongse Zhonghua* (*Red China*), the organ of the Provisional Central Government of the Soviet Republic of China. It was inaugurated in December 1931, at Ruijin, Jiangxi Province. Later it became an organ jointly run by the Central Soviet Bureau of the Chinese Communist Party, the Central Soviet Government of China, the All-China Federation of Trade Unions and the Chinese Communist Youth League. A total of 324 issues were published, including 84 that were put out in Yan'an after the Red Army arrived in northern Shaanxi. Another organ of great importance was *Suqu Gongren* (*Worker of the Soviet Area*), founded in 1933. It actively publicized the Party's policies and tasks, and worked to encourage the broad masses of workers to take an active part in revolutionary struggle. Revolutionary newspapers and periodicals were also launched in the various revolutionary border regions. These included *Hongse Fujian* (*Red Fujian*), provincial organ of Fujian of the Soviet Republic of China, and *Xiang-Gan Hongqi* (*Hunan-Jiangxi Red Flag*), published by the Communist Party Provincial Committee in the Soviet area in Hunan and Jiangxi.

Dangde Shenghuo (*Party Life*), *Qingnian Shihua* (*Truthful Talk to Youth,*) organ of the Communist Youth League of the Central Soviet Area, *Chita Zhoubao* (*Red*

114

Tower Weekly) published by the Youth League Committee of Shanghang County, *Shike Zhunbeizhuo* (*Always Prepared*) published by the Juvenile Bureau of the Party Central Committee, *Qianxian* (*Front*) published by the Political and Military Department, and *Geming Yu Zhanzheng* (*Revolution and War*) published by the Political Department of the Workers' and Peasants' Red Army School were also newspapers and periodicals that catered to the needs of readers among the Communist rank-and-file, youth, and Red Army men. Speedy development was also seen in the publication of books by people in the Soviet areas.

Rough figures gathered in 1934 show that among the 34 newspapers published in the Central Soviet Area, *Red China* ran to 50,000 copies for each issue, while *Truthful Talk to Youth* reached more than 27,000 copies.

The periods of the War of Resistance Against Japan (July 1937 to August 1945) and the Liberation War (August 1945 to 1949) saw steady development in the publication of books related to the progress of the revolution and consolidation of political power in the liberated areas. At Yan'an, the publication of important documents of the Communist Party and the works by Comrade Mao Zedong was taken as the central task of the party's publication work. The newspapers and periodicals published at Yan'an and elsewhere in the liberated areas included *Xinzhonghua Bao* (*New China Daily,* in 1941 renamed *Jiefang Ribao,* or *Liberation Daily*), *Xinhua Ribao* (*New China Daily*), *Ji-Lu-Yu Bao* (*Hebei-Shandong-Henan Daily*), *Taiyue Ribao* (*Taiyue Daily*), *Balujun Junzheng Zazhi* (*Military-Political Journal of the Eighth Route Army*), *Zhongguo Wenhua* (*Chinese Culture*), *Zhongguo Funü* (*Women of China*), and *Zhongguo Gongren* (*Workers of China*). Statistics show that in 1941 a total of 36 newspapers and 38 magazines were printed in the border regions by lead type. All of these had a large circulation. In the case of books, in 1946 the North China Xinhua General Bookstore alone published 596,000 books under 124 titles.

On September 1, 1946, the *Liberation Daily* reported that there were 7 newspapers being published in the Shaanxi-Gansu-Ningxia Border Region, 4 in the Shanxi-Suiyuan area, 1 in the Central Plains area, 6 in the Shanxi-Hebei-Shandong-Henan area, 6 in the Shandong area, 9 in the Shanxi-Qahar-Hebei area, 8 in the Jiangsu-Anhui area and 17 in the Northeast. Incomplete figures show that books and magazines put out by the Northeast China Bookstore in 1946 ran to 903,000 copies in 158 titles. In the Shanxi-Suiyuan Liberated Area, in 1947, the local Xinhua Bookstores issued 184 titles in a total number of 560,000 copies during just the first half of the year.

In the Kuomintang-controlled areas, underground Communist organizations had their own secret publishing houses. In addition, there were many politically-conscious intellectuals who had come under the influence of, or had joined, the Chinese Communist Party. Working through revolutionary cultural organizations, they published revolutionary books and founded newspapers. The League of Left-wing Chinese Writers was formed in Shanghai in the first half of 1930, and this was followed by the founding of the Union of Chinese Social Scientists and the Left-wing Culture Alliance. The members published and distributed a wide variety of literary works that gave publicity to the revolution and heightened the morale of the masses in their struggle against Japanese aggressors and the Kuomintang, as well as Marxist-Leninist works.

At the same time, there were a number of publishers with abundant material resources who channelled their cap-

116

ital into the publication of textbooks for primary and middle schools and into the reproduction of classical works. They produced some voluminous works, such as *Si Bu Cong Kan* (*Encyclopedia of Classical Chinese Literature*), as well as its sequel; *Bai Na Ben Er Shi Si Shi* (*Twenty-Four Dynastic Histories of Miscellaneous Edition*); *Cong Shu Ji Cheng* (*Classified Compilation of Books*); *Si Bu Bei Yao* (*Choice Selections of Classical Chinese Literature*); *Gu Jin Tu Shu Ji Cheng* (*Collection of Books Ancient and Modern*); and *Er Shi Wu Shi* (*Twenty-Five Dynastic Histories*), including its supplement.

After the founding of the People's Republic of China, the publishing enterprises run by the reactionary Kuomintang government were confiscated, and all reactionary, obscene and outrageous books, newspapers and magazines were suppressed. The gradual socialist transformation of privately-owned publishing enterprises was completed in 1956. This transformation brought them into the orbit of the country's planned economy. At the same time, all publishing organizations, both at the central and local levels, were strengthened and augmented, and a professional force was gradually developed to improve the various lines of publication work.

In 1951, the First National Conference on Publishing was held. This laid down the fundamental policy that publishing must be geared to the service of the people. At the same time, the Constitution of the People's Republic of China stipulated that all citizens in the country have freedom to engage in cultural pursuits, including the running of newspapers. Speedy development was thus gained in the country's publication work.

Before Liberation, the total number of books published in the peak year of 1936 was estimated at 178 million

117

copies. But after Liberation, in 1950, the number reached 274.63 million, and in 1953 it reached 748.3 million, better than 4 times the figure for the pre-Liberation peak year. In 1956 there were 1,784.37 million copies of more than 30,000 books published. As to periodicals, in 1953 there were 290 published with more than 11 million copies being brought of each issue. In 1955, there were more than 280 newspapers, among which the country's first leading newspaper, *Renmin Ribao* (*People's Daily*), had a total of 800,000 copies printed of each issue.

But what is more essential to the country's publication programme is the marked improvement in quality of the books and periodicals that are brought out. In old China, publishers were simply interested in money and printed many books of low quality and questionable moral standards. They were also subjected to strict Kuomintang censorship that resulted in deletions from books of all material of a progressive character and the banning of many books. Early in the post-Liberation period, attention was paid by the state to correcting malpractices such as speculation in the field of publishing and printing books in a slipshod way with an eye focussed only on profit. Chinese readers now place strict demand on quality, and comments and book reviews are often published in the country's newspapers and magazines.

But like everything else, publication work suffered during the 10 years between 1966 and 1976, when Lin Biao and the Gang of Four practised autocratic rule over the country's culture. Many publishing offices were closed and their staff members sent to work on the land. Writers were deprived of their right to write, large numbers of books labeled "poisonous weeds", and all works of fine calibre were either curtailed or ceased publications. From 1967 to

118

1970 there were only 3,000-4,000 book titles published each year, and if we exclude picture books and textbooks, there were only 1,000-2,000 titles a year. This created a serious book shortage in the country.

Soon after the downfall of the Gang of Four, in 1976, the Party Central Committee put forward a new policy for publishing. In 1977, a national forum on publishing was called. This specified that the basic tasks for publishing in the new period were: to encourage the publication of books of every description, propagate Marxism-Leninism and Mao Zedong Thought, disseminate and accumulate scientific and cultural knowledge, and enrich the cultural life of the people, so as to help enhance the scientific and cultural level of the entire nation and push forward the country's socialist modernization.

Book publication soon regained its pace of speedy development, and there was a marked increase in the variety and number of books. According to statistics provided by the State Administration of Publication, there were a total of 2,913.99 million copies of 12,842 books published in 1976. In 1980 there were 4,592.98 million copies of 21,621 books published, about double the 1976 figure.

The main developments in book publication in recent years can be listed as follows:

Publication of Marxist-Leninist works and works by Mao Zedong have occupied the first place in China. As early as February 1953, the Editing and Translation Bureau for Works of Marx, Engels, Lenin and Stalin of the Central Committee of the Chinese Communist Party was instituted. Books published by this bureau in Chinese over the last 30 years include the *Collected Works of Marx and Engels* in 49 volumes, the *Selected Works of Marx and Engels* in four volumes, the *Collected Works of Lenin* in

39 volumes, the *Selected Works of Lenin* in four volumes and the *Collected Works of Stalin* in 13 volumes. Also the writings and essays of Marx, Engels, Lenin and Stalin were published in pamphlet form. Soon to be issued will be second editions of the *Collected Works of Marx and Engels, Collected Works of Lenin* and *Collected works of Stalin.*

After publication of the five-volume *Selected Works of Mao Zedong,* the Documents Editing Committee of the Party Central Committee decided to publish works by revolutionaries of the older generation. Those already published include the *Selected Works of Zhou Enlai* (Vol. I), *Selected Works of Liu Shaoqi* (Vol. I), *Selected Works of Zhu De,* and *Selected Works of Deng Xiaoping* (1975-1982).

Many works of philosophy, social science, and science and technology have been published. These include works by such famous scholars as Guo Moruo, Fan Wenlan and Ai Siqi, and scientific works by Li Siguang and Hua Luogeng. Alongside these were many book series and other printed matter on popular science. Statistics show that 5,715 books and 1,384 journals in science and technology, 2,091 books on philosophy and social science (13.3 per cent of the country's total number of books published) and 210 social science journals were published in 1980 throughout the country.

In recent years China's heritage of ancient books has also received a great amount of scholarly attention. The *Twenty-four Histories* in 3,249 fascicles and 40 million characters has been published. This is a series of valuable historical records of the country's political, economic and cultural development, as well as its military affairs and foreign ties over the last several thousand years. In the past, these books were difficult to read and use because of their lack of punctuation and errors in transcription. But now, for the first time in Chinese publishing history, the huge project of correcting and punctuating them in modern style was undertaken and publication was completed in 1980 after 20 years of work. The famous Chinese literary classic, *A Dream of Red Mansions*, was published in its many different editions as were important classics, such as *Choice Blossoms from the Garden of Literature*. These have been brought out in photostatic reproductions of the original manuscripts or in letterpress editions.

Works by famous writers such as Guo Moruo, Mao Dun, Ba Jin, Lao She, Cao Yu, Zhou Libo and Liu Qing have been reprinted. Along with these, a new edition of the *Complete Works of Lu Xun* (annotated), in 16 volumes with a total of 3,000,000 characters, was published in commemoration of the centenary of Lu Xun's birth. The complete works of Guo Moruo in 38 volumes and the complete works of Mao Dun in 40 volumes are presently being edited for publication. Many works by newer writers have also come off the press. In 1979, 59 novels by new writers were published, surpassing the post-Liberation peak year of 1958. The year 1980 saw a total of 3,322 titles of literary and artistic works and 265 literary journals produced throughout the country.

The translation and publication of famous works of foreign literature has been restored. These include the reprinting of works by famous writers such as Shakespeare, Hugo, Balzac and Tolstoy; and the republication, by the People's Literature Publishing House and the Shanghai Translation Press, of the *Marxist Literary Theory Series, Foreign Literary Theory Series* and *Classics of Foreign Literature Series* that were first published in the 1960's.

Another area of active publication is that of books for spreading scientific knowledge and political education among youth and children; as well as dictionaries and textbooks for schools of all types and levels. The best-known reference books are the *Encyclopedia Sinica,* published since 1980 in a series of volumes arranged by subject; and the *Cihai* (*Dictionary of Words and Phrases*) and *Ciyuan* (*Origins of Words and Phrases*), recently put out in new, revised edition. The *Youth Library,* published by the Chinese Youth Press, and *Children's Encyclopedia,* published by Chinese Children's Press, have been well received by young readers. In 1980, 2,446 titles of children's books were published, among which the *Children's Encyclopedia* was issued in more than 33 million copies.

As the demand for printed matter has increased, there have had to be adjustments in the organization of publishing and in the distribution departments. By the end of 1980 there were 192 publishing houses, including 100 national ones.

There is an immense distribution network that extends over the whole country. In addition to more than 7,000 Xinhua Bookstores, there are many bookstalls or book counters in more than 30,000 supply and marketing co-ops in the countryside. Some 100,000 branches of these co-ops also distribute books.

Although much has been achieved in publishing, the rate of production still cannot keep up with public demand. The publishing world, however, is doing everything it can to bring out more good books as quickly as possible, and to raise the level of science and culture among the people so as to expedite modernization.

The Contemporary Book System

When books were first printed by modern methods in China, movable lead type or lithographic stones were used to replace wood blocks. But book design and binding remained unchanged. Thus books appeared to be no different from the thread-stitched books of old.

In the beginning of the 20th century, books with leaves of cap paper printed on one side and bound together with thread stitching were the most common types of books produced. But these did not fit well into a system of modern mechanized printing. Meanwhile, newsprint, book papers and art papers were introduced into China. These new papers allowed printing to be done on both sides of a sheet. Soon the "heart of the block" gave way to a "border title" (book title or chapter head near the "mouth") with page numbers below. Borders were at first kept, but were later eliminated, giving rise to books with paper backs and cardboard bindings as used today. This is how Chinese books, after a long period of development, evolved into their present form. This present form of book binding used to be called "foreign binding", but actually it was an advanced form of the old Chinese wrapped-back binding.

Although there have been a few minor changes since the adoption of "foreign binding", such as the adding of a "brow title" (book title or chapter head) to the top of each page and a page number to the lower mouth corners, and the printing of the author's name, book title and publisher on the spine, generally speaking books have remained as they were when the bound-volume system was first introduced.

Because books with paper backing and cardboard backing can stand erect on a shelf, they present no problem in shelving. People can take them out or put them back on a shelf with ease. This is why it was common in the Song Dynasty for books to be encased in cardboard boxes so that they could stand erect on a shelf. Books in movable lead type can be much smaller than those produced by woodblocks. A bulky work of old that ran to several dozen woodblock books might be printed in one or two volumes in modern lead type. This economized on space, much to the satisfaction of book collectors and librarians.

Almost all Chinese books now read from left to right, as is the case with Western books, which is quite a contrast from the country's traditional vertical method of text presentation. The new system probably began with works in mathematics. In the early 20th century some books on science, mathematics and technology were printed in China with their texts reading from left to right. This was followed by literary works after the May 4th Movement of 1919.

After the introduction of the Chinese phonetic alphabet, in the process of reforming Chinese characters in 1956, many books had their texts printed in horizontal lines. This proved much easier to read when compared with the vertical lines, and so books of this sort were soon put out in large numbers. Greater advantages were also found in printing books with such horizontal-lined texts because they better fit the up-to-date Western printing technology, and this facilitated the development of printing in China.

To paper- or cloth-bound editions, dust jackets of paper are sometimes attached. Printed with the title, author's name, etc., and occasionally with a design and publisher's description, the jacket functions both as a protection and advertisement for the book. Dust jackets are a new form of the ancient "book-clothes". Immediately under the dust jacket is the front cover and back cover of the book, generally with the title and the author's name printed on the front. For a de luxe edition, a blank sheet of paper is placed under the front cover. This is named the flyleaf. It used to be added as a bonding page for strengthening the book body. After this, comes the title page printed with the book title, the author's name and publisher's description.

The distinctions between the various types of books — books with notes, translated works and books in a series — are likewise identified by indicators on the title page. Added to the back side of the title page is a detailed description of the edition, dates of printing, size of format, total number of copies printed, price, etc. Sometimes the back side of the title page also includes the title of the original work, if it is a translation, the names of the editor, designer and proofreaders and that of the printing house. This is, in a sense, the history of the book. After the title page, comes the preface, contents and text, followed by the appendix, postscript and index.

For books published before Liberation, when the country was under a capitalist system all copies contained a copyright page together with a description by the publishers. Today, instead of the copyright page, a detailed description is printed either on the reverse side of the title page or on the inside or outside of the back cover of paperbound books.

中国书的故事

刘国钧　郑如斯

∗

外文出版社出版
（中国北京百万庄路24号）
外文印刷厂印刷
中国国际图书贸易总公司
（中国国际书店）发行
北京399信箱
1985年（34开）第一版
编号：（英）7050—61
00150
7—E—1829P